MW00772555

What Oth
Belly Laughter in Relationships

"Enda Junkins manages to take a serious topic like relationships and remind us that laughter came first...at birth... and then we connect with others. Through her writings, couples can learn how laughter can create a level of acceptance to bond them through the good times and restore them through the difficult times. Sprinkled with anecdotes, this book is a breakthrough in understanding the art of laughing from the belly with one another."
–Lynn Shaw, MSW, LCSW

"**Belly Laughter in Relationships** shows that *love may make the world go 'round, but laughter keeps us from getting dizzy!* Enda helps us look at the love-laughter link while learning ways to transform "serious relationships" into relationships that last with laughter." — **Dr. Joel Goodman,** Director, The Humor Project, Inc., Saratoga Springs, New York

"In my pediatric practice approximately fifty per cent of my patients live in single parent homes. Any approach to lessen the stress of growing up under these circumstances is welcome; Enda Junkins takes a very pleasant look at resolving differences, enjoying life, and keeping relationships fun and vital. Using humor daily with specific exercises may seem forced, but if you'd like to add some laughter to conflict resolution, what better way to communicate with your partner? **–Eric J. Ruby, M.D.,** Board Certified Pediatrician

In **Belly Laughter in Relationships,** Enda Junkins provides an innovative approach for couples to revitalize their relationships. Her creative Laughter Therapy techniques and problem-solving methods not only provide practical solutions to helping couples resolve conflicts but, also, greatly enhance their ability to build healthy committed relationships. This book will provide insight for both professionals and couples. **Patrick Tiner, LMSW-ACP,** Director EAP Services, University of Texas Southwestern Medical Center at Dallas.

"Laughter was one of the reasons we fell in love, thanks for reminding us! **–Helen and Mark**

"It has been said that laughter is the best medicine. As this innovative book so delightfully demonstrates, it is also one of the best prescriptions for making relationships last." — **Allen Klein**, author of **The Healing Power of Humor** and **The Courage to Laugh**

"**Belly Laughter in Relationships** is a unique and revolutionary book. It takes the issues in relationships, fills them with laughter and voila! We have friendships for a lifetime. Enda Junkins provides a thoughtful discussion of the power of laughter in relationships —**Lilly Walters**, Executive Director, Walters International Speakers Bureau and Best Selling Author: **Secrets of Superstar Speakers** (McGraw-Hill)

"Enda's counseling and guidance in Laughter Therapy has brought renewed life and excitement in our relationship and marriage. We have learned new and successful ways to express our true feelings about serious issues and to refocus our energy on our relationship by applying Laughter Therapy techniques. Laughter Therapy has also allowed us to gain a better understanding of ourselves as individuals and as a couple." –**Darlene and Larry**

"**Belly Laughter in Relationships** is one of the only self help books that gets to the real "heart" of the matter, putting fun back into your relationship. The tools that Laughter Therapy teaches you makes it easy to "Fit Fun" into your busy schedule. We would highly recommend Belly Laughter for any couple serious about improving their relationship." –**Jeff and Heidi**

"**Belly Laughter in Relationships** was the perfect book for me to read as I embarked on a new relationship. It reminded me I was making a friend, to find joy in it, and to let the other stuff go. It was a beautiful way to start something and avoid sabotaging in the old way" –**Laura**

"Laughter Therapy really works! When I add humor to the situation, it gives me the proper perspective on the issues I face in my relationships. When your world looks out of control and your problems seem larger than life, I recommend you try "tee hee" and "doodah." –**Randy**

BELLY LAUGHTER IN RELATIONSHIPS

♥ ♥ ♥

Something Else
Positive
Below the Belt

ENDA JUNKINS, MSW

Dustin Royale Publishers
Irving, Texas

Belly Laughter in Relationships
Something Else Positive Below the Belt
By Enda Junkins, MSW

Published by:
Dustin Royale Publishers
3200 N. MacArthur Blvd., Ste. 106
Irving, Texas 75062 U.S.A.
www.laughtertherapy.com

Book design by Richards Creative Imagery

Cartoons by Cartoon Resource at CartoonResource.com, 203-426-1177

Printed in the United States of America

**Publisher's Cataloging-in-Publication
(Provided by Quality Books, Inc.)**

Junkins, Enda
    Belly laughter in relationships : something else
positive below the belt / Enda Junkins. – 1st ed.
    p. cm.
    ISBN: 1-929863-04-7
    Library of Congress Catalog Card Number: 2001118396

    1. Laughter—Psychological aspects. 2. Man-woman
relationships. 3. Interpersonal communication.
    I. Title.

BF575.L3.J86 2002   152.4'2
                           QBI01-201075

To the *Laughing Junkinses* who bequeathed
to my father, Tilford L. Junkins, the gift of
laughter, which he bequeathed to me

And to my mother, Martha Junkins,
who believed in laughter in
relationships until her
death at eighty-three.

Contents

If you don't learn to laugh at trouble,
you won't have anything to laugh at when you grow old.
—Pat McManus

Chapter One
Belly Laughter in Relationships: Something Else Positive Below the Belt

•Laughter Is Part of Attraction • Laughter Puts Us Intensely in the Moment • Laughter Is Marvelous for Love • Laughter Makes It Easier to Cope • Laughter Helps You Enjoy Life More • Laughter Eases Conflict • Laughter Adds Enjoyment to Ordinary Things • Laughter and Humor Are Different • In Laughter We Are Not Alone • Exercise—Belly Laughter for Couples •

ME!?! • SPEAK UP, MY DEAR, SPEAK UP • Exercise—
Speak to Me! Tell Me! Duh, What? •

• Whipped Cream, Silly String, and Sex • In for a Penny,
In for a Pound • Hanging from the Family Tree • A Maid!
A Maid! Our Kingdom for a Maid! • Exercise—Pla-a-ay
Ball!! •

• Living with a Serious Partner • The Search for Laughter
Reborn • Focus on Your Own Laughter • Laughter
Doesn't Change the Facts—It Changes the Way We Relate
to the Facts • A Relationship Is Possible When Only One
Person Laughs • Exercise—Liberated Laughing •

• The Weekly Laughter Workout • Fill Yourself with
Laughter • Laughter Training to Laugh More • Hump Day
• I Love You When You Are Irritating • The Laughter
Sanctuary • The Laughter Reflection • Toning Up Your
Week • Tools, Glorious Tools, More Tools • Laughing and
Loving • Laugh Along With Me • We Laugh Because We
Hurt • Face Off • The Bullet Point Tantrum • Personal
Advisor • Talk To Me, Baby • Love Letters with a Twist •

Foreword

Foreword by Dr. Keith A. Robinson, President
Health Media Network, L.L.C.

It all started when Adam and Eve stumbled onto each other in that garden. From that moment on, man and woman have searched high and low for the secrets that would allow them to live together in harmony. I think it's safe to say that we still have not found the answer...the key to happiness with the opposite sex.

Everything has been tried...we think! Yet, like many breakthroughs, the answer is often right under our noses and has been available to all of us. The question is this: "Will we choose to use something new when everything else we've tried has failed?" Let's hope!

Enda Junkins may have found one of the most important threads necessary to weave the fabric of intimate relationships into a lasting garment of beauty and joy for a lifetime. Who would have thought that humor held the ultimate power to heal the deep wounds left by love gone sour?

Enda draws upon her years of counseling experience, helping couples as they sort out all of the challenges that happen after two people say those fateful words, "I Love You."

In this book women and men alike will find an easy-to-understand presentation on the importance and the necessity for humor in our lives together. We've all experienced people whose face would shatter in a futile attempt at laughter. They go through life aimlessly wondering why people don't love them or want to be around them. This author effectively shows that laughter is an emotional magnet that draws people closer.

So, settle back, and get ready to absorb this delightful book that can't help but open new vistas of happiness in you and in the lives of others nearest you.

Dr. Keith A. Robinson
President/Author/Speaker
Health Media Network, L.L.C.

Acknowledgements

I conceived the idea for this book three years ago, wanting only to help people in relationships have more laughter together, so they could enjoy a lifetime of fun and friendship. I had no idea writing it would take so long. I was also naive about how many different issues are involved in writing a book. I am lucky to have the friends, family, and clients that I have. They were all generous in their encouragement and their assistance.

I would like to thank my sisters, Susan Scott and Annella Flowers, who gave generously of their time as editors to see the book is a good one. I am equally grateful to Patrick Tiner and Sonja Romanowski, friends and professional colleagues, who gave willingly of their time and expertise to edit and proof this book. I also want to thank Laura Murphy who graciously proofed the manuscript and to all those who lent their testimonial to the importance and quality of this book.

I deeply appreciate the opportunity to share the stories of my many clients who were willing to use Laughter Therapy to enhance and heal their relationships. Their stories helped form the book's composite examples that will be helpful to those who read this book in search of revitalization or healing.

I also appreciate the work of my graphic artist, Laura Richards, who helped me create a work of which I can be proud. Finally, I would like to thank my office manager, Carolyn Atwood, who was unfailingly supportive and encouraging and who often helped me to remember to laugh when things got a little too serious. For all of those who helped and supported me, I thank you.

Introduction

Humor is the great thing, the saving thing, after all.
The minute it crops up, all our hardnesses yield,
all our irritations and resentments slip away,
and a sunny spirit takes their place.
—Mark Twain

As a therapist, it strikes me repeatedly as I listen to my clients talk about their troubles just how much we are all afraid to be alone. I don't mean physically alone. It's emotional loneliness we seem to fear most, and our fear seems to spring from the very essence of our being, from some essential element that is part of being human.

I believe we were meant to live with others. Since the beginning of time, people have lived in groups to survive in the environment, and although we no longer need to do this, our genes don't know that times have changed. They constantly push us to find a group to which we can belong and then urge us to find a mate within the group. If we find ourselves without one or the other, we grow terribly afraid that we will be alone—a serious prospect, indeed.

Propelled by the need for a mate and victimized by the belief that we must be gratified at every turn, a huge proportion of us are romping through relationships, one after another. We think that if our relationship becomes too hard, we should leave. Then we begin the frantic hunt for a new relationship because we do not want to be alone.

I am certain that people sincerely want good, lasting relationships. We begin our relationships together with high hopes, caught up in the heart-starting ecstasy of love. We are besotted with one another and never seem to have enough time together. Then, later in our relationships when things slow down some and changes occur, we no longer throb in each other's presence, and we get confused. We've lost something terribly precious but we don't know what, why, nor where it's gone. We start to hunt for the overwhelming love we had and still want, and we begin to view our partners with suspicion. We suspect that they are withholding what we treasure most. We overlook the fact that he or she was once the focus of our greatest happiness.

Without meaning to, we settle into patterns where our lives develop a dry, serious, and unsatisfying quality. We have very little joy and fun. We want these things in our relationships but cannot see that we repeatedly deny them to ourselves. We begin to dwell on the fact that we are not happy, and we think it's somehow our partner's fault.

As a therapist, I have worked with countless couples that are all searching for some way to be happier and more satisfied with each other. Their sincerity and genuine unawareness of their own roles in their problems are always striking. All of them are quite serious about having their noses to the "grindstone of love." They don't play with one another anymore, and laughing together seems to be a ghost of the relationship past. People are generally caught up in serious relationships.

Frankly, I've been there myself. My ex-husband and I loved each other for many reasons, not least of which was an appreciation of each other's sense of humor. We were both playful and found countless ways to have fun together. We laughed a lot and enjoyed each other's company. Then we got married. After an ideal wedding where I remember toasting each other as best friends, we seemed to drop out of the orbit of happiness. We began the serious business of marriage, and slowly the joy in our relationship together disappeared. I am still saddened and disappointed that we finally felt divorce was the best solution. After our divorce, we ironically rediscovered our friendship, and that got me thinking.

It is my belief that it is overwhelming and enforced seriousness in relationships that brings unhappiness and divorce. For many different reasons, we give up a playful attitude toward life together and the laughter it brings. Without laughter, we lose perspective about things so our issues are always "in our face." It's no wonder we eventually want out. We aren't having any fun in our relationships, so there is no pleasure to balance life's expected or unexpected difficulties. We travel from what seemed like total goodness to almost no goodness at all.

I have written this book to draw our attention to the absolute importance of laughter in our relationships. We need laughter to stay attached to each other. When we laugh together, we like and understand each other better. We are more tolerant of each other's shortcomings and that tolerance allows us to keep loving each other. Laughter opens our minds and hearts to one another on a deeper emotional and biological level and helps us maintain enjoyment and approval of one another. Laughter is the oil of life that eases us though the issues that occur in all committed relationships.

In this book, we will explore laughter together as an essential part of relationships. Through examples, stories, and exercises, it is my intention to help you find joy in your relationship with the one you love most. Laughter enriches relationships and keeps them strong and elastic before the forces that challenge our determination to stay together. Deep laughter, belly laughter, truly is something else positive below the belt. As you read this book,

I hope you will "undo your emotional belt" and begin to laugh with your partner at all those things that have seemed so very serious in the past. If you do so, I promise you fun, joy, and a long life together full of friendship and camaraderie. Laughter is a passion for life and consequently allows us to keep passion in our lives together. As you learn to allow laughter to ease you through all the normal issues in relationships, take note of the wisdom of Mark Twain: "Before the assault of laughter nothing can stand."

May you fall before your own laughter and discover your joy in life.

Enda Junkins

About the Author

Enda Junkins is one of the country's leading authorities and foremost speakers on Laughter Therapy. She has spent over thirty years laughing and counseling with others. Enda has personally interviewed hundreds of singles and couples, listening closely to their issues in relationships. For the last twelve years, she has focused on laughter in therapy and developed effective, lighthearted laughter techniques for people to integrate into their lives and relationships.

Enda received her bachelor's degree and master's degree from Baylor University and a Master in Social Work Degree from the University of Illinois. She has applied her professional skills in the practice of psychotherapy for adults and adolescents.

In the past twelve years, Enda has spoken on Laughter Therapy to thousands of people. She has brought her laughter approach into the workplace for issues with stress, communication, employee retention, and as a motivational coach. She has also encouraged the need for more laughter in relationships and has developed the tools to provide it.

Enda has produced three videotapes on laughter and has authored *The Belly Laughter Workbook* for couples.

Enda has lived and laughed in Dallas, Texas for thirty years. She aspires to leave the Texas heat one day in order to live in the mountains of southwest Colorado. She is an enthusiastic sailor and enjoys the challenge of "jeeping" the mountains around Ouray, Colorado. She is an avid "Star Trek" fan and deeply regrets the fact that she will never go into outer space. She remains firmly "grounded" in her speaking, writing, and psychotherapy practice, all of which she enjoys.

Enda's products may be purchased at 3200 N. MacArthur Blvd., Ste. 106, Irving, Texas 75062, (972) 255-LAFF (5233) or at www.laughtertherapy.com.

BELLY LAUGHTER IN RELATIONSHIPS

♥ ♥ ♥

Something Else
Positive
Below the Belt

ENDA JUNKINS, MSW

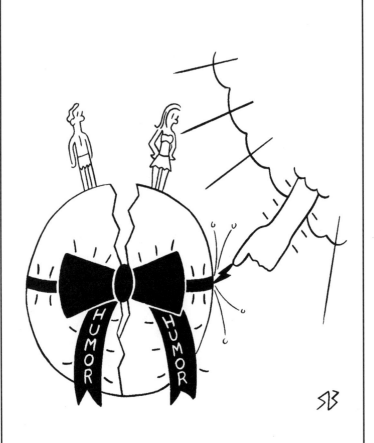

After God created the world, He created
man and woman. And then to keep the
whole thing from collapsing, He created humor.

- Ernie Hoberecht

Chapter 1

Belly Laughter in Relationships: Something Else Positive Below the Belt

After God created the world, He created man and woman.
And then to keep the whole thing from collapsing,
He created humor.
—Ernie Hoberecht

Laughter is in many ways one of life's greatest mysteries. It's common enough that we see it as an everyday fact of life, but we don't really understand it. It is not something that we even feel a need to understand. We just accept that laughter happens, and we like it. We generally take it for granted until it's not around. Then we really miss it.

Sometimes, when I remember the good times in my own marital misadventure, I know that I miss the laughter we shared, and I am sad that I missed its vital significance in prolonging my relationship. As a professional counselor and laughter therapist, I am acutely aware of laughter's importance today and would like to share that importance with you. To set the stage for our discussion, let me take you back to a time in my relationship that I enjoyed but unfortunately took for granted.

One August my husband and I decided to take advantage of the glorious San Juan Mountains of Colorado for a well-deserved vacation. We resolutely let go of our "serious" married life, rented a jeep, and went "four wheeling" for a week. We laughed together a lot as we bounced our jeep over peaks crowded with wild flowers, mountain streams, and waterfalls. We had lots of uncomplicated fun and the laughter that goes along with it.

In our jeep, we climbed high above even the tiniest towns, and as we rose higher and higher, leaving all stress behind, I felt my spirits rise as well. An unexpected laughter started deep within me and then, burst forth for no reason at all. My own joy lifted me up. Perhaps you've had spontaneous fits of laughter much like mine, so you know how wonderful I felt over and over again as my husband and I laughed together for no specific reason. I wish I had valued it more at the time. Had my husband and I known to encourage this kind of laughter in our everyday lives, I believe we could have had a satisfying relationship. However, it was not to be.

Unlike my husband and me, there are people in the world who have been wiser about laughter. I don't know if Ralph Waldo Emerson had ever been to the San Juan Mountains, but he would have recognized the laughter there. He believed that "the earth laughs in flowers" and if that's true, every spring and summer, the San Juans erupt into deep belly laughter, covering the hillsides with hundreds of colorful wildflowers. If even the mountains let go and laugh, it should be a lesson to human beings to follow the mountains' example and allow and enjoy our own capacity for deep belly laughter more often than we do. We also need to value it more for its unique contribution to our lives.

The laughter we casually take for granted is almost magical in the way it impacts us so positively and in the way it adds pleasure to our interactions with others. In light of this fact, it's interesting that we're careless about appreciating our ability to laugh and that we don't laugh more than we do.

It's true, nonetheless, that even though we don't laugh as much as we could, most of us do value laughter, at least on some level. We know it's connected to things that are funny and that it feels good. We don't always know, however, that it is also a serious necessity for good healthy relationships and good personal health. Sometimes it confuses us a bit that something so light can also be vitally important. We don't yet understand why laughter is such a mixture of funny and serious. The contradictions are part of its mystery.

Laughter Is Part of Attraction

> The number one reason for choosing a mate
> is the ability to laugh together.
> —Parade Magazine poll, 1985

What we do know about laughter is that it's a good thing. Most laughter is positive and adds quality to our lives. These are reasons we seek laughter in our relationships. When couples meet, laughter is a big and wonderful part of their initial attraction for one another.

Nathan, for example, goes to lunch with no thought of meeting the woman of his dreams. He and his companions are more interested in their corned beef sandwiches than romance. While enjoying his lunch, Nathan laughs easily with his friends in their corner booth in the restaurant. His laughter catches Madeleine's eye because he looks so pleasant and upbeat. She likes the way he tosses his head back when he laughs. As she watches him, she finds his laughter contagious, and she begins to smile herself. She lights up, and it's as if she has hung a welcome sign around her neck.

Madeleine catches Nathan's attention, and he is attracted by her smile. Impulsively, he approaches. Confident and relaxed by his laughter, he feels good, and he's riding a natural high. His eyes are shining, and laughter still dances in their depths. Something in their smiles and the laughter moments before creates a bond between them, and a new relationship begins.

Laughter makes it much easier for Nathan and Madeleine to meet. Comedian Victor Borge maintained that laughter is the shortest distance between two people. Nathan and Madeleine would certainly agree. Although potential love will find a way without any shortcuts, anything which smoothes the way is a plus. The mystery of laughter and the mystery of love are an unbeatable combination. We're all fortunate that they are intertwined.

When coupled with biological forces urging us to connect with other human beings, laughter makes us feel safer and adds the qualities of fun and playfulness to our attraction for one another. It eases much of our awkwardness and helps us glide through those moments which might otherwise leave us red faced and stammering. Our laughter is contagious, and even those of us who seem inclined to a more solemn approach to life find ourselves drawn into laughing with someone we love.

In addition to talking a lover's talk, we seem to laugh at even the feeblest attempt at humor on our partner's part. By doing so, we give him or her the gift of feeling witty. In addition to giving this gift, without even knowing it, we let go of our own anxieties. Past and current embarrassments evaporate with laughter, and we feel marvelous as a result. When we release anxiety through laughter, our love surges to the surface, and we are able to fully experience and enjoy it. It's a wild and joyful ride.

Nathan and Madeleine seem swept along by forces of nature, caught up in both the pleasure and the intensity of being in love. As they spend time together, they are lift-ed and carried by their laughter, even at the most serious moments. They don't think about it much, but they laugh when they need it most, easing conflict and creating inti-macy. It makes them want to be with each other even more, warts and all. In laughter, they have what may be the only time in their relationship when "the warts" don't matter because they love the "frog" who made them.

Laughter Puts Us Intensely in the Moment

Humor keeps you in the present.
It is very difficult to laugh and be disassociated with people around you.
In that one moment together you have unity and a new chance.
—Alexis Driscoll

Nathan and Madeleine are a young couple in love. Victoria and Bryan are older but caught in love's magic nonetheless. It's somewhat different for them, but not in many ways that matter. After years of serious living, they are loving and laughing once again. They giggle together like school children. Life seems funnier than usual, and their laughter is energizing. What they thought was never-ending fatigue is a memory, and they seem to be riding the crest of a positive wave.

Serious issues are less overwhelming to Bryan and Victoria as they encounter them in a relationship filled with laughter. They are having fun again and feeling great! It's no wonder we all yearn for what we had in the beginning of our relationships. If nothing else, we were intensely alive.

Both couples feel fully accepted by their partners. Laughter has a lot to do with this feeling. Since laughter creates constant perspective, all the uncomfortable traits of our partners seem both unimportant or entirely bearable. We are even able to convince ourselves they are somehow endearing, and we view them with indulgent affection.

Laughter puts anxiety on a back burner for everyone, but especially for lovers. Because we can't laugh and worry at the same time, the future seems far away and less consuming. We are focused on the present and wrapped in a single instant in time. Laughter and love happen in the moment, and hurling caution to the winds, we reach out and seize that moment.

When Bryan looks at Victoria, he only sees how much he loves her. When they laugh together, issues that could be areas of conflict seem less important. Laughter opens many possibilities, and solutions seem to appear by magic. Any need to criticize or analyze has lost its appeal.

Victoria looks at Bryan and also sees how much she loves him. Although the world hasn't changed, she has. She and Bryan laugh over dopey little things like the way his Southern accent sounds over the phone or the way she eats one thing at a time on her plate. Their laughter is almost giddy, and it seems as normal as a cup of coffee to start the day. She snuggles into their relationship, and the world seems far less complicated than before.

When they are together, the many things Bryan and Victoria juggle on a daily basis no longer distract them. They aren't as frantically focused on work, chores, family, and friends. Love seems to have relaxed them, and laughter puts them fully in the moment. They no longer want to keep trying to do so many things at once. They are not preoccupied with other things. They focus on one another. They now realize that they had lost this sort of clarity in the whirling march of details dominating their lives. It feels fantastic to let go for a while and deal with only one thing.

Laughter Is Marvelous for Love

Love has a code name: Laughter.
—David Holmutstrom

Laughter is a marvelous opening for love. It breaks down the instinctive barriers between two people and allows them to trust each other. The fears most of us have about other people are rooted in the past. People have hurt us, and we developed strategies to protect ourselves from any more pain. Our families have also passed along protective beliefs and behaviors, which have evolved over time.

Like Romeo and Juliet, we often have to defy the family rules in order to love one another. Happily, for us, fears and suspicions seem to dissolve in our laughter. The bonding qualities of laughter allow us to feel such emotional closeness that we want to be physically and spiritually close as well. It's something deeper than just biology. It's part of the mystery of laughter that we have yet to solve.

Another special quality laughter brings to relationships is its ability to minimize our need to gain self-confidence by analyzing and judging other people. When we laugh with the person we love, criticism seems to collapse. We are able to let them be themselves and enjoy them even more for that. As laughter opens us up and allows us to be vulnerable, we become willing to make changes. We no longer need to keep score of the good things we do for our partners. We lose track, and we don't even care. Laughter, supporting our love, makes us generous to a fault, and we feel better giving than receiving.

In love, Nathan, Madeleine, Bryan and Victoria are each delighted with the other's differences. Each is inter-

ested in everything about the other. For now, difference
is not a threat but an advantage. Their differences compliment each other, and they feel more complete.

By falling in love and laughing with one another, they
have created a welcome relief from the scrambling to
compete that they generally experience in everyday life.
They feel safe with each other. These four people have
found what we're all seeking—unconditional acceptance.
They have a friend who won't leave and who likes who
they are.

When we're in a laughing, loving relationship, the
hurts we experience in everyday life are not as overwhelming. Our laughter shrinks them to a smaller, if not
inconsequential, size, and we don't have to face them
alone. We have someone to support us and to commiser-
ate with us. As we hold onto one another in times of distress, we grow closer and closer together. As a result,
even distress has its good side.

Bryan can't do enough for Victoria. His laughter has
opened him up emotionally so he can express the love he
feels inside. He doesn't question why he feels so generous and openhearted with her. He accepts the fact that
love creates laughter, and the laughter creates an environment in which his love can grow.

As a man, he has learned to believe that he has to control his emotions most of the time. He has done it for so
long that it has become a part of what he considers his
nature, but loving Victoria creates an exception to the
rule. However, in addition to love, he finds himself coping with other thoughts and feelings as well. He feels
things he doesn't even recognize because they have long
been buried in his unconscious mind. His feelings, creak-
ing a little from disuse, have begun to surface because his
unconscious mind perceives his relationship as a means
for healing old wounds.

Although it can be a little unnerving for him, it also
feels surprisingly good. Feeling means laughing, and he

likes laughing again. At first, he wonders why he ever shut it down to such a degree. Then he is amazed to discover he doesn't care why. He realizes he just wants to let go. When he does, laughter fills him up with good feelings that support his love for Victoria.

In accepting the gift of laughter without question, Bryan avoids one of the major pitfalls curtailing the ability to laugh. Laughter is born of right brain activity and, therefore, lacks reason and defies analysis. It's deliciously out of control because it's not a rational process. Unfortunately, that makes some of us uncomfortable, and we start to question.

When people start to think about their laughter and try to isolate its origin, they stop laughing. Rational analysis is a left-brain function and not conducive to laughter. If we feel we have to offer ourselves or anyone else an explanation about why we are laughing, it is the end of our laughter. Fortunately, couples in love aren't overly concerned with reasons for their good feelings, and, therefore, laughter flourishes.

Laughter Makes It Easier to Cope

> If I did not laugh, I think I should die.
> —Abraham Lincoln

It's always nice when something flourishes which feels good and which serves a positive purpose. This is true of laughter because it helps couples cope with things a little better. They can cope because laughing at problems provides them with a better perspective.

Most of us have a tendency to pay such close attention to our issues that they are eventually a huge part of all we see. If we are able to laugh about our serious things, however, they simply can't be that huge. Being in a relationship often magnifies our unresolved issues, but couples that maintain the ability to laugh about them are better able to roll with the punches.

As a culture, we admire people who are flexible and able to deal with things as they come. It's curious, therefore, that we also have such a strong tendency to focus on things so seriously. Moreover, since serious things require guidelines, we feel forced to make up rules for everything, and relationships are no exception. There are many things we think one should and should not do in relationships. For instance, we should sleep in the same bed and go places in the same car. The man should drive. Women should do the housework and men, the yard work. If we love each other, we should be able to know what our partner is thinking and be able to respond perfectly at all times.

Therefore, as the result of expectations like these, couples tend to make up their own rules about laughter in their relationship. They get some of their rules from their families and some from society, but wherever they get them, they rigorously hold to them. For example, we feel that when we are in an important relationship, we should not laugh about sex or money. They are far too serious. It's a shame, though, because both things are perfect issues for play.

In maintaining this serious approach to relationships, most people have a rule in place which states that problems have to be approached carefully rather than lightly. If you laugh, you don't understand, or you're not a responsible person. There are many more, similar rules to this in our society, and these rules work hard to suppress a couple's willingness to laugh.

All these rules about laughter prevent us from understanding that laughter doesn't diminish the importance of things in the true sense of the word. It simply changes our view of "the importance" so we can feel less overwhelmed and better equipped to cope. Because we find this concept hard to understand, however, we remain reluctant to accept it. Therefore, we laugh less often.

Couples who laugh in spite of the rules, however, stay more comfortable with one another. They are less apt to turn molehills into mountains. Small things stay small, and big things shrink enough to be handled. Kathy and Chris, for example, found their ability to laugh about serious issues to be an advantage when they found themselves deeply in debt. Unforeseen financial setbacks had created what seemed to be an insurmountable problem. They fretted, worried, and found themselves descending into a pit of ongoing anxiety and irritability.

Finally, Kathy couldn't take the pressure of her anxiety anymore. Reasoning that all the worry in the world wasn't going to help them pay off The DEBT, she began to look for a better way to look at the situation. Kathy decided to give The DEBT a name. She began to call it "Bunny" because it kept multiplying.

Then Chris picked up the ball with her, and they both began to talk about Bunny instead of The DEBT. As a result, it became less overpowering. They stopped having nightmares about it and put together a plan to pay it off. They were able to accomplish their goal and have a little fun with it and with each other as well. In an adverse situation, they were actually able to strengthen their relationship.

Laughter Helps You Enjoy Life More

The sound of laughter is like the vaulted dome
of a temple of happiness.
—Milan Kundera

Laughing couples don't worry as much as serious

ones, and as a result, they enjoy life much more. They look for humor in most situations, and that humor provides them with laughter. The laughter makes their circumstances seem less serious and therefore tolerable. When we can see at least some aspect of the silly or ridiculous in what we're doing, we find a solution more easily, or, at least, we buckle down for the ride with less fear and resentment.

Mary and Norman were a couple who could laugh in serious situations. Not long after they were married, they went off on a sailing adventure in the Caribbean. They were fairly new at sailing and had no experience in handling ocean storms. A squall surprised them on a day that had dawned bright and sunny. During the storm, their sails were torn, and they suddenly found themselves staring danger in the face.

While Norman struggled to get the sails down, Mary handled the wheel. She had to steer the boat away from the wind to protect Norman from the wild, snapping lines that could knock him unconscious. To do so, she had to aim for shore. As they moved closer to the rocks, Mary's fear caused her to start laughing. She was pretty sure they were going to die, and it seemed like she was going to go crazy as well. Fortunately, neither catastrophe happened since they were able to get the sails down at last.

Later, as they motored to a safe harbor, exhausted and wet to the bone, they laughed and joked about their brush with disaster. They also laughed at how they would look limping into the marina with tattered sails. Laughing at the humor they found in the situation kept them from being irritable with one another and saved them from ending their vacation on a bad note. Instead, they saw it as an adventure to remember with a smile and a touch of pride that they had met Nature on her own terms and survived.

Laughter Eases Conflict

When you laugh, you can't hate.
—Michael Pritchard

In addition to easing us through trying circumstances, laughter also helps us deal with the disagreements that crop up in relationships because it interrupts the power struggle. It's really hard to lock down in conflict with someone when you're laughing. Conflict is a big problem for people to handle in their relationships, and they often find themselves fighting over things that seem minor in retrospect. Laughter has a magical ability to defuse anger by releasing it. That release, in turn, prevents or stops the conflict, eases the tension, and enables people to see one another's point. Then they can resolve the issue and move on.

For instance, Casey and Dan had been arguing all day. They couldn't see eye to eye on anything to save their lives. They had disagreed about the children, the work around the house, and paying the bills. Each felt the other was unappreciative and had no concept of the stress under which they were operating.

The day before, they had planned to go out but had not yet finalized their plans. Later in the afternoon, during a lull in both the arguing and the chores, Casey asked Dan what he thought they should do for the evening. Without missing a beat, Dan said, "Let's fight." Casey and Dan both burst out laughing. With the tension gone, they were able to decide what they wanted to do without a disagreement to steal away the pleasure.

When couples keep laughing, they can think about what goes on in their relationship. They can see options that are not hidden from view by unacknowledged and

unresolved emotions. They are able to balance the difficulties they encounter with the fun and the good times.
They also remember why they love each other.

We saw this with Kathy and Chris when they named
their debt. In spite of their difficulty with money, Kathy
and Chris never blamed each other for the problem, nor
did they blame their relationship. They stayed in touch
with their love for each other and leaned on each other
for support. They eased the pain of financial strain with
their laughter.

Laughter Adds Enjoyment to Ordinary Things

Humor takes your mind off the negative
and turns it into laughter that's positive.
—Buddy Hackett

In addition to smoothing things out and providing
clarity and balance, laughter allows couples to enjoy even
the mundane things in everyday life. Daily chores are less
burdensome when we laugh while doing them. We aren't
always having fun, but we do have a lot more fun with
laughter than without. It's astonishing just how playful
we feel because we're laughing.

Liz and Tim, for example, had to clean their swim-
ming pool. It had almost reached the point of being a
health hazard. Without enthusiasm, they collected their
supplies, surveyed the pool with dismay, and debated on
where to begin. One of them would have to get into the
water to open the drain. Neither felt like volunteering.

Suddenly inspired, Liz pushed Tim into the water. He
surfaced sputtering and promised revenge. He climbed

out of the pool, growling playfully. He grabbed the squealing Liz and jumped into the pool, pulling her in with him. They splashed around a little, laughing at the way they looked with pool grunge on their faces and in their hair. Then they tackled the actual work of cleaning the pool. Somehow, it didn't seem as awful as it had before.

A playful approach to everyday things in our relationships is a key factor in keeping them healthy. Play is a source of fun, and laughter eases us through those dicey issues from the past. Although we associate play with children, it isn't meant for them alone. Play teaches children living skills, and adults should play for the same purpose. It injects fun into many things that are no fun realistically and helps us do things that would otherwise dismay us.

In his book, *The Enjoyment of Laughter,* Max Eastman comments on the importance of play as "not only something we do, but also something we are while we do it." Play transforms us. Since we feel playful from birth, we have to work hard to give it up. Somehow, though, most of us manage to do it. Fortunate couples hang on to it, however, and they keep laughing. Their laughter leads to more play that leads to more laughter. It feeds on itself.

Laughter and Humor Are Different

Humor allows for a boundary between where we are and some of the cruel things that happen to us.
—Joseph Steiner

We do ourselves a great disservice when we give up play. Then we make matters worse. We confound and confuse ourselves even more by thinking laughter and humor are the same. This results in our need to make rules about when and where we can laugh and what we can laugh about.

Laughter and humor are, in fact, two different things even though they are closely related. Laughter is a spontaneous, physiological process that we all have from birth. As babies, we laugh, but we don't utilize humor. Our sense of humor develops later on. As we grow, we learn what is funny in our homes and the world around us, and our laughter feeds the humor. Humor then, in turn, feeds the laughter. Humor becomes a trigger for laughter. If we see and remember the differences between the two, we won't need as many rules for laughter.

In spite of the differences, it's the connection between the two that makes us search for a lifetime companion with a sense of humor. Humor helps keep us laughing together, and laughter takes us out of our seriousness. Although our important relationships are a vehicle for healing, we can actually have fun along the way. Laughter magically transforms those heavy, hurtful parts of our lives into something lighter from which we can recover.

When we laugh with our partners, we ourselves are fun, and we provide good company for one another. We're able to re-experience something that is at least reminiscent of the unselfconscious silliness we enjoyed when we first fell in love. Since we can't go back to that place in time no matter how much we would like to, we can at least keep the feelings alive. Laughter reminds us of our love for one another, and therefore, we feel it again and again. It's a part of our original relationships that need never end.

In Laughter We Are Not Alone

Laughter is not at all a bad beginning for a friendship,
and it is by far the best ending for one.
—Oscar Wilde

Laughter also provides another bridge to the beginnings of our relationships. When we find someone to love, we feel a profound relief that we are no longer alone. Our primal fear of death by isolation can't withstand our twin defenses of laughter and love, and it retreats into the recesses of our minds. We gratefully relax into the comfort of a companion who loves us and joins with us to create a "tiny tribe" of our own. We no longer live in fear of abandonment.

Laughter is a gift of connection for human beings, and that's why we are drawn to each other when we laugh. When the "new" wears off in our relationships, laughter keeps us caring and supports us as we endure the painful aspects of growth, both individually and together. Laughter is profoundly important in the maintenance of life long relationships.

As a counselor, it is my privilege to enter a very personal place in my clients' lives. I hear tales of relationships lost and relationships found. Laughter is always present in the beginning and always absent at the end. It's a fact that relationships that lose their laughter become brittle and break.

As sad as I am to hear about those broken relationships, it is my pleasure to hear tales of relationships that endure. Without fail, laughter always plays a vital role in that endurance. People report that they continue to like one another because they laugh. They appreciate the ongoing laughter in the relationship and acknowledge its role in easing them through the difficult times.

In my clients' laughter, I recognize their connection with their partners, their friends, and their families. As they invite me into their lives through their laughter, we form yet another kind of relationship, another connection. It seems that our fears of loneliness are mostly "a tempest in a teacup." All we need to fend it off is laughter with another human being.

So—laughter in a relationship is a positive: below the belt, above the belt, and under the belt. It is essential in keeping our relationships alive and well. It will enable us to choose to stay together with gusto instead of resignation.

Now, in order to go for the gusto, the following exercise should get you started laughing. If you've already started, it should help you keep going —so, loosen up those face muscles and get ready for some belly laughter.

Exercise

Belly Laughter for Couples

Stand facing your partner. Place one hand on your partner's arm or shoulder. Place the other hand on your belly (or theirs if you prefer). Look your partner in the eyes and on the count of three begin to laugh. Fake it until it becomes the real thing. Cut loose with your "pretend" laughter so it's deep and belly shaking. After you stop laughing, pause and feel the feelings you have inside. Pay attention to the feelings you have for your partner. Enjoy them a moment and then share some of these feelings with one another. Wind up with a nice, warm hug. If you begin and end your days this way, your relationship will benefit and so will you.

It is bad to suppress laughter.
It goes back down and spreads to your hips.
—Fred Allen

Relationships are too important to be taken seriously.

Chapter 2

In Our Face

What is simple about a love that is destined to last
seems to hang on the ability to laugh together
at anything, including each other,
with a sense of timing and concern
that has not a shred of cruelty.
—David Holmutstrom

Steve woke up one morning with a sinking sensation in the pit of his stomach. He looked at Dawn, his wife, and wondered, who is this person? He could barely remember her as the woman he fell in love with. In some ways, she seemed like a stranger.

This wasn't the first time he'd felt this way. On other occasions when he felt dissatisfied in the relationship, he had looked through their photo albums, seeking some sort of reassurance. In the moments captured by the camera, he saw two people obviously crazy about each other. It's amazing, he would say to himself. Those people are us. In almost every snapshot, he and Dawn were laughing and having some sort of fun.

This morning he found himself musing about fun. Where did it all go? he wondered. We used to really like each other, and just being together was fun. Now we're serious all the time. No wonder people call marriage The Old Ball and Chain. Sighing to himself, he rolled out of bed to another serious day. Steve had no idea how to reawaken the joy in his relationship nor where to go to find out how.

Laughter and Fun Are Essential in Relationships

A well-balanced person is one who
finds both sides of an issue laughable.
—Herbert Prochnow

Steve and Dawn's situation is, unfortunately, not all that rare. Relationship after relationship bites the dust because the couple no longer has fun. Of course fun is not all a relationship is made of, but it's much more important than we realize. The fun we have together shores up the more serious aspects of living with another person for a lifetime. The idea of doing anything for a lifetime causes many of us to have our eyes glaze over in boredom. If we can visualize a rollicking good time over the long haul, we're more apt to enjoy and cherish what we have instead of exploring elsewhere to see if we missed anything.

Love, support, acceptance, commitment, and friendship are just a few of the serious things we seek from our partners. Think about it. How often do you talk about serious things with the person you love while laughing and smiling? We usually discuss these wonderful, positive aspects of a relationship while wearing our most solemn faces and using our most sincere, serious tone of voice. We often say I love you with the same sort of gravity reserved for a judge sentencing a prisoner to life at hard labor. We seem to have misplaced joy and excitement—much more suited to the power of love—on an emotional back burner.

The more intense we become about the serious things, the more we need laughter to help us succeed in giving and receiving with pizzazz. It's strange how somber we can be about a relationship—the same relationship we used to enjoy as much as a small child savoring an ice cream cone. Once we wore the creamy mustache of love around our mouths and dripped the excesses of total satisfaction onto our T-shirts. Now we attempt to enjoy this same relationship with a prim, controlled kind of enjoyment that just doesn't work.

Take sex, for example. It's often no longer a spontaneous roll in the hay. It's not even a planned roll in the hay. If we're relaxed enough to be in the hay at all, we have to create neat little piles of hay in which to roll. Then, afterwards, we carefully remove all signs of hay from clothes and hair lest someone suspect we've had a little fun in an undignified way.

The Biological Love Bug

Laughter is "good stress" in the way a passionate kiss is. It excites us and makes us feel great.
—Paul Rosch, M.D.

I suppose the reasons we have relationships could be viewed as serious. If, in the beginning, however, our relationships felt serious, it would be interesting to see how many of us would follow through. Actually, we jump into our relationships reasonably unaware of three important reasons driving our actions.

First, we find ourselves biologically triggered by the other person. Our hormones activate, and our five senses launch a love campaign to motivate us to capture the interest and affection of those to whom we are attracted. We begin to feel the most astonishing things.

The chemicals we produce in our bodies like pheromones, dopamine, norepinephrine, phenylethylamine (PEA) and adrenalin create just the right amount of desire balanced with doses of physical pleasure. Naturally, we want more, and we can be almost consumed by this desire. Fortunately, nature did not intend us to languish in the "opium den" of lust. Our bodies also release other, more dignified, chemicals like endorphins and oxytocin that create warmth and caring between us and the people we love. They are released by all kinds of touching that bring us closer and actually create bonding. The chemicals also enhance our memories so we'll linger in each other's minds.

According to science, the natural drug cocktail produced by the body can't be sustained much longer than two or three years. We actually develop a drug tolerance to our own biological chemicals and no longer have the love buzz. We're lucky to have it that long, so we have to turn to other means of keeping our relationships vibrant and growing.

Bonding Through Laughter and Touch

In friendship let there be laughter
and sharing of pleasures.
—Kahlil Gibran

It is encouraging to know that after our bodies stop naturally producing these "love drugs," we can still keep the bond strong with touch and with laughter. Both produce endorphins that bring us pleasure and reduce stress and anxiety. You could say that ongoing love is a natural form of stress management in a relationship. Nevertheless, as important as touch is in love, laughter still takes pride of place in keeping people together.

Barbara Bush, the wife of President George Bush, told *Life Magazine* that humor and the laughter it creates have kept her union with George a strong one. It stands to reason that if laughter can help a relationship survive the rigors of the Presidency, it's the glue-all to end all. Therefore, if we keep lots of laughter in *our* lives, it can help us stick together long enough to mend anything that's broken.

Laughter and touch both create bonding between people and encourage long-term relationships. Science has learned that touch creates this bond by releasing the chemical oxytocin into the body. Chemically, regular touching keeps us close, and closeness minimizes criticism.

There's a proverb that wisely points out that *Kissing brings two people so close together, they can't see anything wrong with each other.* If you find yourself "locked up" in criticism in your relationship, perhaps you should grab each other and start kissing. Do it by surprise, and it should create laughter. If you add the bonding qualities of laughter to the bonding qualities of touch, you will be able to form a long-lasting, satisfying form of "bondage" with your partner.

We Seek to Be Whole

Laughter is the shortest distance between two people.
—Victor Borge

In addition to biology, we are attracted to our partner because he or she seems to possess qualities we admire, but lack, in ourselves. For example, our partner may be emotional, funny, and outgoing while we are stoic, serious, and shy. We seek the balance he or she offers us. It's possible we once had the same qualities as our partner but set them aside for reasons long forgotten. Whatever the case, the person makes us feel whole.

All of us are born with all systems on green. We are loving, emotional, creative, imaginative, intelligent, and playful, and if encouraged to grow and develop to our fullest capacities, we would feel whole. However, since we all have very human parents with issues and needs that quite naturally impact us, none of us grows up intact. We develop some qualities and repress others because it makes sense in the families in which we are raised. Somehow, in all this, deep down inside, we never quite lose the knowledge of what we once were nor the yearning to feel as complete as we did at our birth.

Since we don't consciously know we are seeking to be complete, we are unaware that the missing parts of ourselves attract us to other people, especially the person we love. When we connect with them, it feels like scratching an itch. Oo-oo-ooh, it feels good! We get a sense of completion and think we have found our soul mate—or perhaps I should say our "whole mate."

We Need to Resolve Old Issues

Humor arises directly from the process of perception
which allows the mind to switch over
and look at something in a completely new way.
—Edward de Bono

The final reason we choose to love this person who initially seems to be perfect is that he or she reminds us of our mother and father. We don't choose a mother-father figure because we are strange in some way. We do it because love presents a new opportunity to resolve old hurts from childhood.

For example, if you grew up the youngest in a large family, you might choose a mate who is a good listener. You anticipate that the person will listen to you with rapt attention at all times. This attention will make up for the times Mom and Dad were too busy to listen when you were a child. Some inner wisdom is guiding you to help the child inside stop that desperate yanking at Mom's apron to get her to hear you. Understandably, most of us are not thrilled by the idea that love can have this or any other kind of hidden agenda. Therefore, you might find yourself wishing that your mind were not so solicitous of your mental health.

Nevertheless, we invariably choose a variation of Mom and Dad when we fall in love. No matter how wonderful our parents were and are, no one emerges unscathed from childhood. Since there are no real parenting classes and we don't have to be licensed to be a parent, all moms and dads make mistakes. Meeting all of each child's needs is a monumental task, and busy parents just can't meet all those needs. It doesn't matter how much they might want to do so. Therefore, we grow up with a nagging appetite for more attention, approval, love, touch—whatever need went unmet in childhood.

When we're children, we find ways to do without all of the things that we need, and we put them on hold until a later time. Then, when we arc adults, our unconscious minds are constantly on a healing quest, trying to help us take care of all those frozen needs.

Our mind is like a ship with a sailor on watch in the crow's nest at all times. When the lookout spots a potential source of needs gratification, he sings out, "Needs, ho!" We then change course to zero in on the person who is an attractive, interesting, potential whole-mate. Our new whole-mate will unknowingly serve as a substitute for our parents. We bring our ship of needs along side, lock on with grappling hooks, and happily prepare to board or be boarded. The needy part of us begins to wiggle in anticipation of having our needs met at last.

We Love Because It's Fun

This is what it's all about:
If you can't have fun at it, there's no sense hanging around.
—Joe Montana

In the beginning of all our relationships, the factors of biology, wholeness, and needs gratification are unconsciously in place for both partners. They are the snap, crackle, and pop that keep things interesting. In addition to the intrigue inherent in all relationships, the person we love dazzles us in his or her own right. What is unconscious is unknown to us, and even if we knew, we would not care. Loving someone is fun, all consuming, reckless, and supremely human. Confident it will never end, we join the other person and move forward toward our future.

Even though we realize this relationship is important and one of the more serious undertakings of our lives, it doesn't feel serious. Everything seems colored by playfulness, and we are creative in our interaction together. Even the ordinary stuff like eating, sleeping, and hanging out together is fun. There seems to be no end to the imaginative ways we develop to play and laugh together. We give ourselves permission to have all kinds of uncomplicated fun. Like children, we might slip our hands over the other person's eyes and say, "Guess who?" Adult versions of Peep Eye can have us rolling on the floor, and boisterous, playful hugs make our day.

Serious things are still happening on a daily basis, but taken playfully in love, they don't seem to matter as much. We laugh at little serious things, and we laugh at big serious things. For the time being, we agree with Oscar Wilde that, "Life is too important to be taken seriously." It's a time when we allow our instincts to help us go with the flow.

What Happens to All the Fun?

So long as there's a bit of a laugh going, things are all right. As soon as this infernal seriousness, like a greasy sea, heaves up, everything is lost.

—D. H. Lawrence

One might think it's easy to miss the seriousness in life the way we work to keep it right there before us. The truth is that it's almost impossible to overlook the seriousness of important events and issues. It's also true that people tend to bear up better while dealing with such things when a little humor and play are present to lighten things up. They enable us to take care of things without struggling to carry them as if they're a ton of bricks. Laughter is an essential part of living. When we find someone to live with that we can also laugh with, we're lucky, and we know it.

Many of us seem to lose all our joy somewhere along the way. The loss happens to us unconsciously, seeping into our relationships so gradually, we fail to notice the changes. Then, like our friend Steve, we see it all at once and feel hammered by life itself. We look at our partners with an eye to criticism. We notice all their flaws, down to the smallest detail. We feel deliberately cheated by the fact that they are no longer making us happy. We have stopped kissing. We are locked in a power struggle for love and have no idea how we got there. The *tingly* feeling of anticipation we used to feel is now the *prickly* feeling of irritation.

Tom and Kimberly haven't been married for a very long time, but things have already gotten prickly. The biological high that usually carries a couple through the first "honeymoon" year or two wore off quickly for them. After only two years, they are totally bewildered by the fact that even the little things in their everyday lives have become a big deal. They seem to argue about unimportant things like which cereal to have for breakfast, who works the longest hours, and who started the last argument. They even argue about who argues best by presenting his or her case most effectively. All the things they disagree about are constantly in their face. Even the things they don't disagree on somehow shift into issues that make them want to hurt each other. They are in such a fight mode that agreement feels surprisingly uncomfortable— the calm before another storm.

Take Tom, for instance. Tom doesn't really think when he debates with Kimberly, and she doesn't either. Their mouths are open, but their brains are closed. They both know, beyond a shadow of a doubt, that they are right about everything. Each loudly claims to have a verbatim memory of every conversation. Of course, in their minds, the other one does not. They tend to share their superior total recall whether it's welcome or not and see their partner as too stupid to see or remember his/her own mistakes. Each of them yearns for the other to see the error of his ways. All they want, they say, is for their partner to be "more like I am."

Kimberly shows her frustration more easily, but she still laughs when the absurdity of what they both say and do strikes home. Tom, on the other hand, is totally and unyieldingly serious. In his mind, he is reserving his laughter for something funny. He refuses to laugh or admit that anything he says could be the slightest bit unreasonable. He bores into every situation like an electric drill boring into a wall.

Both Tom and Kimberly want to be happy with each other. They want to have fun again but don't know how to break free of their ongoing battle. They finally seek counseling to save their relationship. They know they still love each other but can't bring themselves to show it or feel it. They find it really tough to want to stay with each other when everything in the relationship is sour and heavy. This is understandable because being with another person needs to be fun at least part of the time to be satisfying.

Although marital counseling is a serious endeavor, Tom and Kimberly found laughter in therapy to be life saving. They were up to their eyeballs in serious squabbles and needed to lighten up to even begin to break free. They agreed to try laughter techniques like yelling "I love you, Sweetie" at each other instead of yelling hurtful things. They also learned to playfully channel their complaints by lovingly saying such things as "You know I married you because I knew you would be the most irresponsible and irritating spouse I could ever find" or "I love you so much for all your faults."

Playing with the issues they were serious about finally broke them out of their anger. For example, they created certificates of merit for working the longest number of hours in a week and had a presentation ceremony each week. Both hung CW certificates on their wall and laughed about being proud of being a Certified Workaholic. They also voted on the Cereal of the Week, and they had a little ceremony on Monday. It made it fun to think they were eating a prestigious cereal. As they began to see the folly of their situation, solutions began to present themselves. Slowly, laughter began to sound throughout their home once more, replacing the rumble of angry thunder.

When couples enter a power struggle and let playful-

ness drop by the wayside, they lose touch with their laughter and very often with their love. That's what happened to Tom and Kimberly.

The Power Struggle for Love

Laughter removes the burden of seriousness
from the problem, and oftentimes,
it's that very serious attitude that is the problem itself.
—Bob Basso

When we lock into the power struggle, we start to annoy each other. We totally focus on our own needs and blunder about, knocking into the needs of our partner but having almost no inclination to meet them. The very things we liked so much about our partner in the beginning now get on our nerves. It's interesting how we almost completely forget how we once liked their "irritating characteristics."

Our soul mate becomes an alien stranger. They mess up our neat houses and track mud onto spotless kitchen floors. They smack their gum, and the sound of their breathing keeps us awake. They talk too much, or they talk too little. They chew their food too loudly, leave the toilet seat up, and fail to replace the toilet paper when it is empty.

They also have opinions of their own that always seem to conflict with ours. They spend our money and eat our food. The blinders appear to have finally dropped from our eyes. We are amazed that we entered into a relationship with one whom we now consider the dumbest, most irresponsible, selfish, boring, person we could find. In addition to all this frustration, we feel irritated that we still love them.

The more irritated we become, the less flexible we want to be. We lower our heads, hunch our shoulders, and charge. We utterly flatten playfulness and its accompanying laughter. We are angry most or all of the time even if we don't know why. Our unconscious minds have caused us to clash head on. We focus on our needs and our needs alone. We want what we want when we want it and think if our partner really loves us, he or she will give it to us.

We don't do these things purposefully, nor are we even fully conscious of our motivation. If we were, we could see the contradictions and the humor in what we complain about. Human beings do not glide noiselessly and spotlessly though life. There is truth to the television commercial that announces, *Life's messy. Clean it up*. It does not say, *Your partner's messy. Make him or her clean it up*. We are all messy and imperfect. If we stay playful, we learn ways to adjust and help each other clean it up.

As we adjust to our partners, those little nicks we find in our behavior can just as easily be hooks on which to hang our love instead of our criticism. For example, in the movie, *Good Will Hunting*, Robin Williams' character nostalgically and lovingly remembers his deceased wife's tendency to fart in her sleep and then deny it. These are the details of intimacy, and it is possible to appreciate them—believe it or not.

We Can Be Playful While Seeking the Love We Need

Humor is the instinct for taking pain playfully.
—Max Eastman

It's ironic that we choose to fight when our minds are

trying to help us heal our old wounds and meet all our old needs. Just when we need it most, we no longer play: we do battle. But, if as it seems, battle must be joined, why not do it with a touch of playful exaggeration? If it doesn't work, you can always duke it out seriously at a later time.

To try a more playful approach, first choose a current bone of contention like the toilet seat up or down, lights on or off, smacking gum, or breathing too loudly. Pick the appropriate arena. A toilet seat dispute should take place in the bathroom for example. If your level of irritation allows it, you might playfully announce yourselves as if you're in a professional boxing ring. "Ladies and Gentlemen, in the window corner, we have Tom, Long Time Champion for the Toilet Seat Up!" "In the sink corner, across the hole, we have Kimberly, Ladies Defender of the Right to the Toilet Seat Down." " Fighters, keep to the rules, fight fairly, and let the fight begin."

The two of you then begin to take turns pushing the toilet seat up and down with appropriate battle statements and sounds. You might say things like, "Take that, you toilet seat leaver-upper, you," "Seat up rules!" or "My arm, my arm, it's so tired of lowering the seat." The fight ends when one or the other can fight no more. At the end of the battle, you should be laughing, and some perspective about the issue will be imprinted on each of you for life. You may also become aware of the real, deeper issue, whatever it is, and find a solution. Of course, you may also have to buy a new toilet seat.

The Fight for Happiness

Joy is not in things, it is in us.
—Benjamin Franklin

When locked in the miserable struggle to feel more

loved, we draw on all our emotional and intellectual weapons. We agonize and obsess over why we have to do things his or her way. We dig in our heels. We tell ourselves we have to fight back. We think we have to fight or we won't get what we need.

See if you can picture two 300-pound NFL linemen facing each other across the line of scrimmage. In this case, NFL stands for Not Fair Loving. These two ferocious athletes of love are determined to tackle any effort on the other's part to cross the line to get their needs met. They are totally focused. The rest of the players can do what they want. Our two linemen see only each other and the need to stop one another. They believe that if they fail, they will never be happy, and the game will be lost. Pushing and pulling, sweating and grunting, they achieve a stalemate.

Coaches send in play after play, and, to their frustration, the two linemen continue to make the same block and tackle over and over. Finally, however, even their mighty strength begins to buckle. To each of them the solution seems so simple. If the other person would just do things right, if he or she would just love in the right way, all would be well. Each of our linemen is certain the other is the problem. All one has to do is convince the other of that fact, and he or she will surely change. Then we think the "Happy Game" will be won.

Yelling Is Telling

Where there's laughter...there's hope.
—Comic Relief, 1990

In this battle for love, each partner sets out, unconsciously, to make the other love him in the way he needs to receive it. When it's not forthcoming, wives and husbands harangue each other, thinking that nagging, yelling, and pleading will surely bring the other around. We need to think again. Yelling almost never works. Being battered by words makes us hunker down inside, clench our jaws, and become determined to resist to the bitter end.

And another thing—Perhaps we think we shouldn't tell our feelings to anyone. All of us were warned not to tell at some time in childhood. We learned that our childish telling could get us in trouble, so we began to keep our own counsel. As adults, we value privacy, and almost all of us keep some things secret. So, when we yell about our differences, we are actually telling. Yelling is telling, but no one is listening. It's been said that the only people who listen to both sides of a family quarrel are the next-door neighbors.

An alternative to yelling could be the following lighthearted approach. It's a problem-solving method that can be used in lieu of talking your partner to death by debate, pleading, or screaming. First, identify the issue at hand like washing dinner dishes, not enough romance, or paying the bills. Now try to turn the issue into a lighthearted debate. One will be for, and the other against. A variation of this approach is to argue your partner's point of view.

Let's choose Washing Dishes BT (before television). During the debate, make your case with as many silly, made-up facts and statistics as you can come up with. For example, couples that wash together, stay together, or statistics show that when one partner does more dinner dishes, the overall IQ of the relationship rises. This increase is due to the fact that the other person is gathering information from TV shows. Try to keep your facts and rebuttals to 2 or 3 minutes. Points are scored each time a debater gets a laugh from the other. The one with the most points wins.

After such a debate, each of you should see the other's point much more clearly than if you made it yourselves, seriously and loudly. The laughter and play will allow you to hear each other and really consider the other person's point of view. You should then be one step closer to some sort of resolution.

Silence Is a Golden Opportunity

As soon as you have made a thought, laugh at it.
—Lao Tsu

Some partners fight by withdrawing into silence. Silence is a powerful weapon remembered from childhood, and we use it on our partners in self-righteous indignation. All they have to do to regain our favor is become exactly what we tell them to be. In our silence, however, we nurse our grudges and grow further apart, distancing ourselves from love.

Some of us grew up in such a way that we have a terrible time resisting the use of silence either as a safe haven or as a weapon. If such is the case, it's time to accept our silence and use it to bond instead of distance. We can do so with the following exercise.

In order to use silence for bonding purposes, two partners must first agree that silence must not include physical withdrawal as well. When one retreats into silence, the other must follow whether he wants to or not. All communication from that point on must be nonverbal. To communicate on an issue, you will use pantomime. You must reach any resolution nonverbally. If no issue is identified, after 30 minutes of silence, one or both partners must move to make positive physical contact.

Contact can be as simple as a hug or a kiss. It can, and hopefully will be playful. Have some ideas for physical contact already ready and listed somewhere in case current circumstances curb your creativity. A playful example of physical contact might be taking a strand of last night's spaghetti and eating toward the middle from opposite ends. When your mouths meet, have a hug and a kiss before you start chewing.

You might decide to sit down at the opposite ends of the couch and move closer bit by bit until you're snuggling next to one another. Put an arm around each other so you're connected and then continue to sit in silence. When silence is so uncomfortable it no longer works, break silence and talk things over. You will find you feel safer as well as closer.

Let Me Tell You

> I think the next best thing to solving a problem
> is finding some humor in it.
> —Frank Clark

Some of us like to lecture each other to try to get what we want. We point out the error of our partner's ways in the treacherous world of loving another person perfectly. We tell them how to do it, how our parents did it, and how our friends are doing it. We point out their selfishness and how harmful it is to our relationship. We go on for hours, utilizing adjective after adjective to describe the art of loving someone, especially when we **are** that someone. The sad result is that we still do not get the love we want.

However, if you just can't resist lecturing your partner, try *The Laughing Lecture* first. There is always a chance to go back to the real lectures at a later time. You might try two variations. One form of lecture is limited to one minute and is called *The Sixty-Second Silly Sermon*. Write out a list of your critical adjectives for your partner and after the first one put ha, the second one ha ha, and so on. Your list might go like this: lazy, ha, stupid, ha ha, irresponsible, ha ha ha. By the time sixty seconds are up, your perspective will have shifted, and a balanced discussion can take place.

The second variation of *The Laughing Lecture* would be to insert "ha ha" after every critical word or statement in your lecture. For example, you could say something like this: If you were more courteous, ha ha, you would call when you are going to be late, ha ha. You never think about anyone but yourself, ha ha. I always call you when I'm going to be late, ha ha.

This method of lecturing will take out the sting of the words and give both of you a better look at the issue. It will not diminish what you have to say or what you feel. It will actually help the other person really listen to what you have to say because the anger and criticism are lightened. You both have a much better chance at continuing to feel loved by the end of the serious discussion.

If you feel a little resistant to any or all of these alternatives, it's perfectly normal. We tend to approach our fight for love very seriously. Treating it lightly, even for the short term, goes against the grain. Getting the love we need is as "serious as a heart attack" to most of us and may well give us a heart attack the way we currently handle our feelings.

Love Without Lunacy Is Impossible

Start every day with a smile and get it over with.
—W. C. Fields

It's hard to see anything humorous or contradictory in any of our behavior while engaged in the power struggle. Whooping and hollering to make someone love us is irrational, but we tend to miss the irrationality. Perhaps in the wisdom of a Yiddish proverb, we will see ourselves: *Lunacy without love is possible. Love without lunacy is impossible.*

Edward and Ann Marie were masters of lecturing and criticizing each other. Where once they saw intelligence, wisdom, and warmth, they came to see self-absorption, lack of consideration, and stupidity. In between attacks on one another, they tormented themselves with questions. Why am I doing this to the one I love? Why can't we enjoy each other the way we did in the past?

Sometimes, when there was a break in the emotional pushing and pulling, they had a great time and briefly remembered the things they liked about each other. Truce was rare, though, and they were always driven back to the battle front almost against their will. They still laughed on occasion as their bodies involuntarily released their feelings through laughter, but they seldom played together.

Their salvation came during a moment of truce. When looking for camping gear, Edward went shopping at an Army-Navy store. While browsing around, he came across the combat helmets. Momentarily inspired, he bought two—one for himself and one for Ann Marie. Then he went to the toy store and bought two "ray guns" that made loud, funny noises when fired. When he got home, he presented his idea to Ann Marie.

He proposed that, in their next argument, they don their helmets and pull out their ray guns. With each angry outburst, they were to fire their guns as well. As the ray guns fired, and they looked at each other in army field helmets, something shifted. They no longer saw an enemy. They saw someone they loved with whom they were having a disagreement. Soon lectures and constant criticism became less frequent, and play came back into their relationship. They liked each other all over again.

Hello Mother, Hello Father

A good sense of humor helps us in many ways.
It helps us understand the orthodox,
tolerate the unpleasant, overcome the unexpected,
and survive the unbearable.
—Gene Brown

The power struggle sneaks up on us because the person with whom we fall in love and form a relationship is something like our mother and father. How we resist that idea! We want our relationship to be unique and unconnected to the past in any way. We don't want to create a relationship with our mother and father. We've been there, done that. We want something special that is ours and ours alone. Our unconscious mind, however, has other ideas. It wants us to heal those old hurts, and our love relationships are the means it chooses to help us do it.

So, against our will, we are faced with the fact that our partners are our mother and father in ways we never suspected. It's hard for us to see it, but we can certainly feel it. We also respond to it. We determine to make our partners love us at least as well and hopefully better, than Mom and Dad. That will fix all those yearnings we have felt for so long. We expect them to make us happy all the time, but it doesn't work that way. They want the same thing, and they have equal power.

Our struggle for power to get our needs met, no matter what, never accomplishes its goal. The result is a stranger in our beds and in our lives. Home is no longer a safe place to be, and we're not having any fun. We're in a very serious relationship and it's always in our face. Life doesn't have to be that way, however. Good relationships, important relationships, don't have to be serious. No matter what we're working on unconsciously, we can still have fun with each other, and we can even have fun with the issues themselves.

Laughter and Play in a Serious Relationship

To be playful and serious at the same time is possible, and it defines the ideal mental condition.
—John Dewey

It is possible to keep laughter and play in our relationships on a regular basis. Having laughter and play in our relationship will prevent us from locking down with our partners in the power struggle. We will still go there on occasion, but we do not have to stay there. There are people who manage to keep in mind that their relationship doesn't always have to be a somber affair, and we can be one of them. Your sense of humor and your laughter can rescue your relationship regularly if you let them. As the saying goes, "Angels can fly because they take themselves lightly," and if you take yourselves lightly, you can have an "angelic" relationship.

Maintaining a playful approach to life and looking for and enjoying the humor that abounds can provide us with wonderful, soul-saving laughter. Our laughter eases us through the tough times that even the most devoted couples face off and on. It helps us face our own neediness and releases the pain we still carry from childhood mishaps that were left unresolved. If we really want to Get Over It, as we are so often told to do, laughter will help us do it. Our humor is an intellectual way of playing with things. Humor, coupled with creative ideas and behavior, joins with laughter to help us enjoy a riot of a relationship.

If You Take Life Too Seriously, You'll Never Get Out Alive

To be in love is to be in play.
—Sir Thomas More

Elbert Hubbard reminds us, tongue in cheek, that "If you take life too seriously, you'll never get out alive." The following three couples are among the lucky ones who figured that out on their own. For whatever reasons, they have been able to allow themselves to laugh about serious things and approach them in a spirit of playful attention.

In addition to admiring the child present in all people, these couples nourished this wonderful, survival mechanism in themselves and in their relationships. As a result, they have been able to navigate safely through the challenges presented by normal, everyday living.

The combination of laughter and play and its relationship to survival and problem solving is something uniquely human. When we allow it to operate as intended, so many things become richer, and we feel the balance of life playing out within us.

According to Thomas Moore, *To be in love is to be in play.* Helen and Jack would agree with that quote wholeheartedly. They have been able to keep their relationship healthy without having to stay serious most of the time. They are playful with each other on a regular basis, and that playfulness spices up their marriage. One of the ways they play together is what they call The Joys of Stranger Danger. They take turns calling each other unexpectedly and pretending to be a stranger who is totally besotted with the one being called. Sometimes they enrich the call by adding accents or different personas, like schoolteacher, CEO, or movie star.

For example, Helen might call Jack and leave a message

in a breathless, sexy, yearning voice: "Jack, you don't know me, but when I see you leave your office everyday, my heart begins to flutter, the blood pounds in my ears, and my legs turn to water. Your wife must be luckiest woman alive." Whatever may be going on in Jack's day is enhanced or minimized by such a positive message. A smile crosses his face and is written in his heart, and his love for Helen grows just a bit more. By playing this way, Helen and Jack maintain the fun in their relationship, and they remember and renew their love for each other regularly.

If our need to be loved is one reason to seek out relationships, ongoing support is certainly another reason that is of equal importance. A light touch for all kinds of things, even serious issues like losing a job, financial problems, or terminal illness enables us to provide that support mutually without feeling overwhelmed or overburdened. Bud and Linda, for example, found themselves faced with the very daunting task of dealing with Bud's diagnosis of terminal cancer. Although they coped in many other ways as well, they found themselves playing with the process of living with his cancer and laughing as a result.

One day, Bud was in the kitchen making himself a snack. Little things were frustrating his efforts, and he allowed himself to get into a real snit. Hearing him griping and snarling at his snack, Linda who was seated at the kitchen table, leaned back in her chair and said, "Bud, life's too short for this—especially yours." They both laughed, and life went on. Other people didn't always understand their laughter and were sometimes critical. For Bud and Linda, though, the laughter they shared right up to the end added to the quality of their relationship and to the quality of Bud's life while he lived.

In addition to approaching serious things playfully, seeing the humor in situations that aren't the least bit funny can be a lifesaver. Humor can also preserve our dignity—a need for relationships and the people in them—both internally and externally. Cliff and Alice, now in their 80's, have used and enjoyed humor throughout their long marriage of well over 50 years. Humor has saved them from the seriousness of situations many times, and Alice's stay in the hospital for minor surgery was no exception.

After surgery, when Alice needed to go the bathroom, she was afraid she wouldn't be able to make it in time because of her infirmities. Improvising, she decided the situation called for emergency measures. Thank God for plastic trash can liners. She lowered herself onto the trash can, going for the short-term solution. Somehow, she lost her balance and found herself sitting, bare-bottomed, on the cold, linoleum floor.

Cliff tried to help her up, but because of his severe arthritis was unsuccessful. They did then what they had always done so often. They laughed at their predicament. Then feeling somewhat better, they devised a solution to the problem. Alice helped Cliff pick her up and get her back into bed. Cliff tidied up, and together they preserved dignity for them both. Once again, laughter saved them from what could have been a mortifying moment. It also helped them cope with an awkward situation created by illness and age.

By playing and breaking up the stress of an ordinary day, playing with serious issues, and finding humor in situations that aren't funny, these three couples kept fun, life, and health in their relationships. Without having to work at it, they expressed and appreciated their love. When emotional needs and misunderstandings threatened to create a problem for them that could have resulted in a power struggle, they were normally able to power on through and keep their balance as friends and lovers.

All couples can follow these examples. There is never a need for a relationship to be so serious that it is always *In Your Face*. Regular doses of laughter and play take the work out of staying in love for a lifetime. Your laughter will let you take your relationship out of your face and keep it in your heart instead.

Exercise

On Our Face

We often don't realize that the looks on our faces have lost the love that was once mirrored there when we looked at our partners with our hearts in our eyes. It is very possible to regain those loving looks so the blah, angry or dirty looks we don't even know we're giving are replaced.

This exercise can just be a game of taking turns making loving looks at each other and allowing our partner to guess what we're thinking. The idea is similar to that of children making faces at each other to see who laughs first. The fact that it's been so long since we've worked at showing our love on our faces and that it's being done deliberately will probably bring laughter. If not, it will at least create warm feelings between you. Once your partner guesses the type of face you're making, share the thoughts and feelings that go with it.

You can add a more developed game-like quality to the exercise by listing different types of loving faces on slips of paper and drawing them one by one. Then act them out as charades. Your list might include loving looks like moonstruck, calf-eyed, glazed, adoring, sweet, intense, drooling, and worshipful. You can create as many types of looks as occur to you and your partner and friends. This exercise can be done by the two of you or with others as a type of parlor game. Share the thoughts, feelings, and events the charade represents.

You can each then draw a simple picture of the loving look you most want to see on the face of your partner. Stick it around in different places as a gentle reminder to each other to remember to look as if you love each other. The picture can be silly or just a light touch to keep your relationship lively. After the entire exercise, share with each other how it felt to give and receive loving looks and hear the thoughts and feelings that went along with them. Tell each other how it feels to see a simple, cartoon-like drawing of the look you most long for sticking around different places. It will be easier to consistently show love on your faces as a result.

Humor is an important part of a marriage.
Sometimes you have to break the tension
with a joke or a look.
—Bob Newhart

Chapter 3

Dance with the
One Who Brung You

Laughter need not be cut out of anything
since it improves everything.
— James Thurber

Karen stared into the mirror. Why, the tear-stained eyes demanded, do you keep choosing the wrong guys? Even as she yielded to the wash of self-pity, another part of her stepped back, looked at the entire pitiful scene and laughed. In spite of her misery, the laughter burst to the surface. She sank to the floor laughing hysterically. "This isn't funny," she howled but laughed until she lay exhausted on the bathroom floor.

As she lay there, she asked herself, "What would Lucy on *I Love Lucy* do in this situation?" Laughing again, she decided Lucy would give herself a face-saving reason for her disaster, set her sights on a new, even more unlikely man, shift her creativity into high gear and go for the brass ring one more time. Encouraged by the thought and amused that she might be the only person in the world with Lucy as a hero, she allowed her mind to wander.

As she pondered the lessons on life and romance in *I*

Love Lucy, she suddenly heard her grandfather's voice saying one more time, "Listen, Girly-Girl, if you want to make a go of a relationship, you should always dance with the one who brung you." Karen smiled at Grandpa's folksy wisdom which gently urged her to focus on her partner and try, try again instead of deciding to dance with someone else because it is easier. I wish I had followed his advice, she thought, instead of giving up my relationship with Bill impulsively. In my next relationship, Karen said to herself, I will go for the brass ring, and I will see it through to the end. Then, she got up and prepared for a new day.

The Survival Pattern

The best way to deal with imperfection
is to laugh at it...especially if you don't plan to change it.
—Joyce Saltman

Karen's new resolution was a wise one. There is no magic relationship-pill to save us from difficulties in relationships. If there were, people would eat them by the handful. The reality is, if you don't work your issues out in one relationship, you will do so in the next. Here's the reason why.

All of us develop ongoing patterns of behavior as we grow up in our families. We do what we do because it helped us get along with our parents and our brothers and sisters. These patterns become second nature to us and operate entirely on autopilot. The "shoulds" and "should-nots" that tell us what to do are rooted deep in our minds. As a result, we are unaware that we're in a pattern of behavior at all. We think our behavior is the same as our personality and our character and see it as unchangeable. It's scary to try to change something so deep, and therefore, we defend ourselves against criticism and change by saying, "That's just the way I am."

Our perception that these characteristics are unchangeable often sends us into despair and sends our relationships into the divorce courts. However, there is no need for these situations to happen. Most of what we consider our identity or "who we are" is really a series of learned behaviors or "what we do." It's encouraging to know that what we learned we can unlearn if we really want to do so. We don't have to give up and leave the "one who brung us." With a little more concentrated effort, we can keep on dancing together and do it joyfully.

The Mind Says Work It Out

You can turn painful situations around
through laughter. If you can find
humor in anything...you can survive it.
—Bill Cosby

Although working out our past and present psychological issues with our partner can be difficult, the mind has decreed it will be done. We add to the difficulties ourselves by somehow viewing and living life together as a project. We start doing life a particular way and assign each other duties. For instance, it's my duty to cook and yours to clean up. I'll pay the bills, and you wash the car. We will clean the house together. In "doing" life, we forget to enjoy life together and to appreciate each other's company. It's when we take on life as a joint project instead of a joint adventure, that our relationships lose their pizzazz. We need to "wake up and smell the coffee." If we don't make an effort to "live" our lives instead of "do" them and work out our past issues with our current loved one, we will eventually have to do so with the next, the next, or the next.

Karen, for instance, grew up with a dad she adored. He was also very self-centered. She could never satisfy him completely on anything. As a result, she never felt "good enough" as a child. Consequently, each time she formed a relationship as an adult, she chose a man who was self-centered. They were not all as selfish as her father was, but they were unable to give her the attention and approval she craved. So, as it developed, her pattern of behavior in her relationships was either to take care of her partner so he would love and approve of her, or she would refuse to meet his needs at all. This survival behavior of hers invariably triggered her partner's defenses. Then, his survival defenses would trigger her defenses, and they played out conflict after conflict.

As miserable as the power struggles were for Karen, she could never see her situation clearly. She lost her sense of humor, and she and her partner weren't able to laugh and have fun together. All they could see were their unmet needs for approval.

Unfortunately, Karen wasn't one of the lucky ones. The lucky people manage to remain instinctively playful in their relationships. When their patterns threaten to block their good feelings for each other, somehow, they manage to maintain a light approach to the situation, or they are able to lighten up about it relatively quickly. As painful as Karen's search for approval was, it didn't have to be as serious as she made it. Even though her insecurity wasn't funny, if she had used an exaggerated, playful phrase like "I'm good, good, good!" when feeling a need for appreciation, the tension between her and her partner might have lessened. Then, she and her partner could have avoided or worked through at least one of the roadblocks created by unmet needs.

The Determined Ones

A smile creates another smile.
A smile is the first step for humor to be possible.
—Alex Port

Lucky for us, we don't have to be one of the lucky ones to keep play and laughter in our relationships. We can be one of the *determined ones* and make a determined effort to laugh and play our way along life's path together. Issues are a part of life, and we all have them in spades. It's how we deal with them that counts.

Statistically, the average couple spends ten minutes a week in play. You need to increase that amount by at least six times or more. You played together in the beginning of your relationship to increase and maintain your attraction to each other. You can resume your play now and continue forever. It's an important approach to weave into your relationship. If you need a few ideas to get you started, try these: Greet each other after work with a "shimmy" saying, "I love you, love you, love you." Use some word play about chores like "I hear the garbage calling to me, saying take me out, take me out." Hug each other with enthusiasm like two lovers meeting at the airport after a long separation. When you learn to think playfully and lovingly and act accordingly, laughter and joy will be your reward.

There is a reason that we stop our romantic silliness after we're in a relationship. Our mind seems to catch us by surprise in its attempt to guide us to greater emotional health. Our mind is delighted when we find someone to love. It smacks its lips at the juicy opportunity it now has to work out some old issues from childhood. As a result, we begin to interact with our partners the same way we interacted with our parents. Weird as it may seem, our "partner scenario" is pretty much the same as the "parent scenario" with just a few modifications.

The ancient Greek gods were supposed to have played with the emotions of humankind. Perhaps the gods also created our unconscious minds to reenact our pasts in a lighthearted, teasing attempt to keep us balanced. Unfortunately, in relationships, both partners do the same thing at the same time, and thus begin a "dance of behavior patterns" that can cause great distress if the two remain unaware. The mind's attempt to provide the gift of health can turn into disaster.

Our distress causes most of us to get serious about the issues, and we find it hard to keep perspective. Laughter helps us lighten up and allows us a balanced view of things. If we know about patterns of survival and approach them with laughter and humor, we can eliminate some of the issues that crop up repeatedly between partners. We can also learn to break free of the patterns bit by bit. Clarence Darrow, the famous attorney, believed that "you may defy all the rest of the rules if you can get a man who laughs." He applied that belief in the courtroom, but it is also true in relationships. Laughter helps us break through the rigid rules laid down by our behavior patterns and do things differently.

Maria and Jeff had been married a while when they found themselves locked in a dance of patterns. Maria grew up never feeling good enough. She worked extra hard to be good enough at work, at home, and with friends. Jeff also grew up feeling criticized, but he developed the opposite pattern. He didn't try very hard to please anyone but felt deeply hurt if anyone pointed it out.

In their relationship, Maria took care of Jeff's needs and never allowed him to help her. She desperately wanted his approval. Secretly, however, she was angry that he did not help even though she refused his occasional offers to help. Because she wanted approval so badly, she never let him know her real feelings. Then, since Jeff was habitually critical, she never got the approval she craved, and she felt unloved as a result. Jeff also felt unloved because she never seemed happy with him. They picked at each other in their own ways, and the criticism/unloved scenario played out repeatedly. They both felt miserable but had no clue as to how to change the situation and put love and laughter back into their relationship.

Then, they discovered how to become part of the *determined ones*. At a marital seminar, they learned how to identify their patterns and find ways to play with them. When one was being critical, for instance, the other would put a smile on his or her face and say, "Thank you so much for the criticism." This particular tool began to give them perspective. Maria learned to playfully ask for help by throwing her hands up repeatedly and saying, "Help me, help me, help me, I'm drowning." Once they began to play with the issues, their creativity came to the rescue, and they came up with some outrageous, fun ways to lighten things up.

When the issues seemed lighter, Maria and Jeff became more flexible and more positive. They slowly but surely stopped their chronic criticism and consciously began to put fun back into their relationship. They did simple, sometimes boisterous things that created uncomplicated good times. They consciously unlocked the tension from their facial muscles, and they laughed more. Then, as they integrated more laughter and play into their daily lives, they found approval and acceptance right where they left them. It is possible to get back the wonderful feeling that you are okay in the eyes of the one you love. To remind themselves of this, Jeff and Maria framed a quote from the Sewanee Mountain Goat that said, "Marriage is an institution. Marriage is love. Love is blind. Therefore marriage is an institution for the blind."

Identifying Patterns Can Be the Key

Like a welcome summer rain,
humor may suddenly cleanse and
cool the earth, the air and you.
—Langston Hughes

In trying to regain that loving feeling for each other, identifying your patterns can be helpful, even crucial. Being able to identify them without censure can be a bit tricky, but you can do it. It will make a huge difference. The relief at being able to stop banging your head against that unchanging wall of irritating behavior compares favorably to the aftermath of an explosive orgasm. Every part of you gets to relax at last.

Paul and Felecia had been banging their heads against each other's behavior for quite some time. Paul's pattern was to either seek approval or totally stop caring. He found himself married to Felecia who had the common pattern of either taking care of others or doing nothing for them at all.

Normally, when Paul sought approval, Felecia found it easy to take care of him. She gave him the approval he craved. She felt very nurturing and very successful.

However, when he stopped caring, she found it harder to take care of him. She then felt helpless and frustrated because she couldn't help him, and she was apt to flip over to wanting to have nothing to do with him. He then felt unloved, and she felt angry and cheated of the man she thought she married.

They could have stayed serious about the situation and locked down in unhappiness. However, the better choice was to find a way to play with the situation. By choosing to play and laugh about their issues, they could open up a wide range of options to handle things. They would have a smorgasbord of solutions instead of one, two, or no solutions.

So, Paul and Felecia decided to play with what was happening. Since it seemed to trigger most of their conflict, they decided to confront Paul's pattern of not caring instead of avoiding it. They started by playfully calculating lighthearted ways of not caring like eating all the chocolate chip cookies alone instead of sharing, belching openly and loudly, and scratching themselves in public. They mixed the sillier ideas with more straightforward ways of being uncaring and made a long list. Doing this simple thing increased their awareness of the pain of acting uncaring in their relationship in a way that seemed less overwhelming. They began to gain some perspective that would allow them to make changes.

Realizing that not caring is connected to negative thinking, they used the game "Some Days You're the Bug; Some Days You're the Windshield" to try to combat the tendency to focus on things that are bad. When playing the game, their premise was that you don't care which one you are, "the bug" or "the windshield." They played both sides of each issue by looking for good things about being the "bug" and good things about being the "windshield." Of course, the game can cover a wide variety of good and bad situations, which can be turned into good/good situations.

To lighten her frustration about Paul's negative view of life, Felecia began finding ways to exaggerate the idea that everything was worthless. Paul was slowly able to join in. They found and explored worthlessness in many good things like winning the lottery, taking a cruise, getting a raise at work, the children all getting straight A's, and so on. Their creativity provided them with a lot of fun, and some of their ideas were downright hilarious. They were laughing a lot more.

Then, Paul and Felecia went even further and researched the potential worthlessness of life. They even drew a few worthless cartoons to depict the worthlessness. They rented all the worthless movies they could think of, saturating themselves in so much worthlessness that it became funny to them. They also listed the good things about apathy and stuck the list on the refrigerator. Out of all this overdone worthlessness came a new appreciation of worth, right down to the little bitty things in each day.

Paul found himself responding to the play in spite of his innate resistance. He began to see reasons for caring more and how his pattern was denying him joy in living. He and Felecia would playfully argue about which things to include on the list of good things about apathy and found a whole range of lighthearted reasons to care. They no longer bogged down in the serious aspects of everyday life as often as they once did.

Felecia recognized her mom and dad in Paul's behavior, and he saw his parents in her. Therefore, they playfully decided to celebrate their anniversary with dinner for six, the two of them and both sets of parents. Paul and Felecia progressively learned to play with their patterns whenever they recognized them and to use humor to unlock the behaviors. As a result, they were able to enjoy their differences and offer each other more approval and appreciation. Their growing awareness of their patterns also made them more tolerant of each other's behavior. They stayed more aware that the other's irritating habits were not the same as the person themselves. They saw their behavior as something they did, not who they were as people.

The Patterns of Childhood

Lots of laughter and a sprinkling of love—
as far as we know,
that's the best way to deal with anyone.
—Lynne Alpern and Ester Blumenfeld

Although like Paul and Felecia we are all born with great flexibility and many opportunities, life causes these choices to narrow. It is somewhat like a Musical Chairs version of life. We start out with lots of chairs or options, but each time we hear the music stop, we lose a chair. Finally, the process stops at two chairs or options. When it becomes only two choices, we have developed our survival pattern. In the pattern, we choose to sit in one chair or the other most of the time. For example, we sit in either the chair of trying to please or in the chair of being displeasing. We even have a favorite choice, moving to the other choice only occasionally. These patterns develop in response to our living situations and serve to protect us as children. Their development is not a measure of how good or bad our parents were. It is simply the way of things in the world of childhood survival.

As children, we tend to develop our behaviors in response to our parents' behaviors. The patterns that evolve may include both the positive and negative traits of our parents. Like it or not, we are like our moms and dads in certain respects. For example, growing up with parents who are perfectionists could cause someone to develop the pattern of "Either I'm perfect or I'm a failure." A person with this pattern is usually in hot pursuit of an elusive perfection and doomed to failure in the pursuit. Since we know perfection is not possible, failure is the inevitable result even if the thoughts and feelings only take the joy out of what would have been perfect otherwise. It's difficult to find happiness if one operates in this particularly painful, no-win pattern.

When we are operating inside our patterns, we do not feel our feelings. The pattern protected the child we were from feelings he or she didn't understand and couldn't process. In the simple way of children, we developed choices that became either/or. This black and white way of looking at things to determine a course of action works well for coping with the overwhelming issues of childhood but can do us harm as adults. As adults, we have the ability mentally and physically to consider and choose from many more options which may be more appropriate than the ones allowed by our patterns.

Over time, the pattern locks in for children and becomes automatic. It doesn't shut down when we become adults. It is all-powerful in the child's life, and its rules are rigidly enforced. Because it is automatic and unconsciously driven, it causes us to act in ways that don't always make sense for an adult. Therefore, our patterns "wag the dog" in a manner of speaking. We act a particular way even when it is not in our best interests.

For example, a controlling pattern can keep an argument going for a lifetime about who initiates sex and how. This pattern needs to be in charge in order for its person to feel safe, and it needs the partner to give in to its wishes. The pattern causes the argument to continue by keeping pressure on the partner. It does this even though the issue is not important in the grand scheme of things. Few people will feel regret on their deathbed over how often they initiated sex with their partner. Imagine yourself dying and whispering to your partner of a lifetime, "I'm so sorry I didn't initiate sex with you more often." It doesn't make sense, does it? Nevertheless, the pattern keeps the issue serious and ongoing even when it's senseless. It is still trying to protect the child by doing things the same way over and over, always striving to be in control.

In addition to causing us to do things that don't make sense, the ingrained pattern has a whole host of ideas and beliefs that support the resultant behavior. These become the reasons we give others for doing what we do. This is the pattern's verbal line of defense. The reasons are the same in adulthood as they were childhood. We simply change the words to protect the adult from feeling silly.

A child, for example, might say, "I want my own way because I want it." The adult would say, "My way is better because it's more effective, easier, or right." We continue our childhood patterns after their usefulness is over because they are a deeply ingrained habit, and they defend themselves vigorously. It is from their defense that marital wars are born. Survival and defense are huge issues for couples and any pressure to change triggers serious anxiety and resistance. As a result, male and female armies take the field over things like affection, approval, trust, and respect. Too often, these armies take no prisoners.

Frozen Needs

A smile is a curve that sets everything straight.
—Phyllis Diller

As our childhood patterns cause us to fight with one another, our lingering needs from childhood cause us to seek satisfaction from our partners. We want them to love us, approve of us, support us, listen to us, hold us, and so on. However, no matter how hard our partner may try, he or she cannot give us all of what we need. Nevertheless, we want them to!

Since no one met our needs completely when we

were children, they froze that way in time. Our partners, no matter how hard they try, can only help meet our adult emotional needs. We must meet the frozen needs from childhood by our own efforts to know and satisfy ourselves. To find satisfaction in a relationship, we have to try to understand how frozen needs fit into our patterns and into our partner's patterns. If not, we tend to fixate our frozen needs on our partner and drive each other crazy criticizing our inadequate attempts to meet them.

For example, if we have an approval-seeking pattern and our partner does also, we need to realize that we will probably never get enough approval from each other. Our unmet childhood need for approval is frozen in the past. To try to get that need met by our partner will only create a stalemate on the battlefield for enough approval. However, by recognizing that we can't get all we need from our partner, we can try other ways to deal with it like laughing about the discomfort, focusing the need elsewhere or even overdoing it with each other in an exaggerated fashion in order to gain perspective. If we can begin to see our patterns of behavior as something that covers up who we are instead of being who we are, we can keep our connection to each other as people instead of giving up in disgust or despair.

If we become aware of the many ways that each person's pattern dominates his or her life, we can identify and try to change the self-defeating parts while keeping the good parts. We can work to replace the discarded behaviors with healthier, helpful ones. For example, Paul was able to replace his tendency to view things from a helpless, apathetic point of view with a healthier interest in how he could change things that were bothering him.

Identifying a Pattern

The most wasted day of all is that on which
we have not laughed.
. —Sebastian Roch Nicolas Champort

By now, you may be interested in identifying your pattern and that of your partner. The following exercise will be helpful in doing so.

1. Write a list of all the things you <u>always</u> do or you <u>never</u> do. Include all areas of life like work, social, child-rearing, dress, food, sex, play, and relationships.

2. Identify the most common motivation for the things you do. They might be things like approval, fear, selfishness, lack of trust, need for love, appreciation, anger, self-sacrifice, revenge, etc. You can do this by asking, What is my motivation for this particular always or never behavior?

3. Then identify the core behavior the motivation creates. Examples of behaviors caused by the underlying motivation might be: control, perfectionism, demanding, nurturing, self-sacrificing, interrogating, or withdrawing. Asking how you keep the always or never behavior going should help you identify the core behaviors.

4. Once you get a consistent behavior like controlling, for example, write down a pattern statement and fill in the blank. The first part of the state-

ment will be about the behavior. Make the second half of the statement the answer that pops into your mind after you say the first half. I'm either controlling or I'm_____.
These will be the two extremes of your behavior pattern. You can do this with your partner and help each other identify the "always or never" things you tend to do.

Sample Version of
Paul and Felecia's Worksheets

PAUL

Always

1. Always asks for reassurance that his decisions are okay. For example, he asks Felecia if what he tells their son to do is acceptable.

   Motivation—needs approval. *Behavior*—asking for approval.

2. Always tries to do things the way others want him to do them. Before tackling a task, he will ask detailed questions about how the other person wants it done.

   Motivation—needs others to like him. *Behavior*—seeking reassurance.

3. Always tells people what he's done well so they will compliment him. He might brag to a friend about working out, for example.

   Motivation—needs approval and appreciation. *Behavior*—seeking approval.

4. Always supports his behavior by saying other people think it's good too. He might explain that he mows the grass a certain way because all the guys he's talked to say the grass stays healthier that way.

   Motivation—avoiding disapproval. *Behavior*—defending against criticism.

5. Always researches anything he does beforehand so he can be comfortable that he will do it right and others will approve. He might check out the facts on all big screen TV's before he buys one and tells anyone about it.

   Motivation—need to be right and good. *Behavior*—studying details to avoid possible mistakes.

6. Always pouts and says "whatever" if he is criticized.

   Motivation—need for approval. *Behavior*—pouts and does nothing at all.

Never

1. Never initiates a plan of action, i.e., where to go eat, what movies to go see, etc.

   Motivation—fear of disapproval. *Behavior*—won't pin self down.

2. Never does a thing on impulse like buying a new shirt or sending flowers for no reason.

   Motivation—fear of doing the wrong thing. *Behavior*—always behaves predictably.

3. Never says what he really thinks.

   Motivation—scared of saying the wrong thing. *Behavior*—indecisive and quiet.

4. Never offers new information for fear it will be wrong. He waits for someone else to offer an opinion and agrees or disagrees depending on whose approval he's after. For example, if Felecia says a 401K loan is a good deal, he will agree and even pass her reasons on to other people.

   Motivation—fear of being wrong. *Behavior*—repeats other people's opinions and ideas.

5. Never takes risks like doing things at work an entire-

ly new way. He always follows the tried and true way.

Motivation—fear of disapproval or failure. *Behavior*—behaves predictably.

After reviewing his motivations and behaviors, Paul concluded that seeking approval was the most common motivation. He then developed the following pattern statement.

Pattern Statement

Either I'm seeking approval or I just don't care.

FELECIA

Always

1. Always takes care of other people's needs instead of her own.

   Motivation—need for love and approval. *Behavior*—nurturing.

2. Always makes a concerted effort to praise people even if she's not sure they deserve it.

   Motivation—need for acceptance. *Behavior*—nurturing.

3. Always helps other people with their work.

   Motivation—need for love. *Behavior*—nurturing and helpful.

4. Always volunteers to do others' tasks for them, particularly if they are finding it difficult.

   Motivation—need for love and approval. *Behavior*—self-sacrificing.

5. Always thinks about Paul's schedule before agreeing to do something for herself.

   Motivation—fear of confrontation and loss. *Behavior*—self-sacrificing.

6. Always defers to her husband even when she disagrees.

   Motivation—fear of loss of love. *Behavior*—supportive and self-sacrificing.

7. Always shuts down when she is very angry.

   Motivation—fear of confrontation and loss of love. *Behavior*—withdrawal.

Never

1. Never puts her own wishes first.

   Motivation—need for approval. *Behavior*—self-sacrificing.

2. Never sets aside time for herself.

   Motivation—fear of loss of love. *Behavior*—self-sacrificing.

3. Never stays out long with friends because she feels guilty about her family.

   Motivation—fear of disapproval. *Behavior*—self-sacrificing.

4. Never buys herself anything frivolous without first checking with Paul.

   Motivation—fear of confrontation. *Behavior*—avoidance.

5. Never allows herself to confront anyone.

   Motivation—fear of loss of love and approval. *Behavior*—avoidance.

After reviewing her motivations and behaviors, Felecia concluded that the behavior most common to them all involved taking care of others. She then developed the following pattern statement.

Pattern Statement

Either I take care of others or <u>I leave.</u>

Other Examples of Pattern Statements

Your pattern may not be listed here since this is a short list of examples. There are many, many different types of patterns developed instinctively by each individual child to suit his or her situation.

1. Either I am controlling or I am passive.
2. Either I become what others need me to be or I am totally nonconforming.
3. Either I take care of others or I take care of myself.
4. Either I seek approval or I leave.
5. Either I am very loving or I am hateful.
6. Either I am selfish or I am generous.
7. Either I am seeking appreciation or I attack.

Survival patterns, several of which are identified above, pervade every area of our lives. We learn to do it when we are young, and it becomes second nature over time. As mentioned earlier, along with the pattern itself, we develop a rigid set of thoughts and beliefs that support or explain our behavior and make it acceptable. We also develop subpatterns like alcoholism, overeating, overspending or overworking to support the pattern as well.

It is important to remember that our survival patterns originally developed as a good thing and helped us manage our feelings as a child. They also kept us safe. Therefore, when we operate within our pattern, we still feel comfortable no matter how miserable it makes us. The pattern's primary purpose is to keep our emotions numb and under control. Because it operates unconsciously, the behavior it generates is not our fault. We are responsible for what we do, but that doesn't mean we do it on purpose. Therefore, blaming each other for what we do is not helpful or appropriate. Even though Mark Twain believed that "Nothing so needs reforming as other people's habits," trying to force our partners to change is a no-win proposition. Each person must want to change and work at those changes daily, or it will never happen on a permanent basis.

Playing With Patterns

He who laughs, lasts.
—Norwegian proverb

Since patterns are not generally funny, you may be wondering what they have to do with laughter. Knowledge allows one to play, and play creates laughter. When people have the knowledge to identify the patterns in themselves and their partners, they can find ways to play with them. The more couples can play with the behaviors they both indulge in, the easier it becomes to make changes to accommodate each other. Laughter makes change less daunting and more fun. People are more apt to take action when it's not heavy, cumbersome, or expected.

Paul and Felecia's playful solutions to each other's often irritating behaviors were described earlier. They immersed themselves in worthlessness and devised many creative ways of looking at the problem of negativity and apathy. Each individual or couple can find ways to play with their own situation. The following exercise is a helpful tool for seeking out our pattern's impact on our everyday lives. It also provides items to play with and gives one direction.

1. Draw a circle and put the pattern statement in it.

2. Draw rays extending from the circle like a sun.

3. On each ray of the sun, write one behavior in your everyday life that the survival pattern causes. Look at every aspect of your life: family, marriage, social, work, children, dress, food, driving, play, etc. Let's look at Paul's diagram as an example.

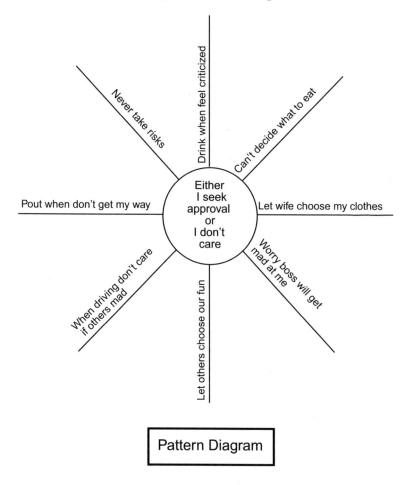

Never take risks

Drink when feel criticized

Can't decide what to eat

Pout when don't get my way

Either I seek approval or I don't care

Let wife choose my clothes

When driving don't care if others mad

Worry boss will get mad at me

Let others choose our fun

Pattern Diagram

Begin with a simple diagram. Also, try to think of it as a fun diagram. If you make this too hard, you won't do it. You just want to get yourself started. You can always add to it later. Once you identify behaviors to put on the rays of your sun diagram, you have areas with which to play. This makes it not only possible but also easier to change the things you want to change. If certain things are too hard to change, the laughter and play will shrink the issues and make them manageable.

After you have completed your diagram, list the items on the rays of the sun on a piece of paper. Devise a way to be playful with each one and write it down. After devising ways to play, pick one item and play with it until you have it down pat. Then, move on to another. Remember that you can't just do this once and expect to succeed. You have to do it repeatedly to change the habitual behavior you have used for so long. If each of you does this, many of your conflicts will ease or disappear.

It is also helpful to compare your pattern with your partner's pattern and then highlight the problem areas where the patterns fail to fit together well. For example, a caretaker might have an issue with an approval-seeker who tries to get approval by caretaking. They will probably fight over who gets to take care of whom since they both need to be the caretaker to feel comfortable. Focus your play on your areas of conflict in addition to the behaviors listed on the diagrams. The play can open up new solutions. Please don't worry about playing too much. A balance will always occur within the play itself. The laughter will help you work your issues out a lot easier and have a little fun in the process.

Playing with problems only takes a little creativity and lots of flexibility and willingness. It also takes perseverance. By playing, you are trying to change a serious habit. Therefore, even if you have to sigh and "suck it up," force yourself to have fun over and over again. There are many ways to play with issues. For example, if the woman talks too much and the man talks too little, practice reversing roles. Set aside five minutes where the man must talk and ask questions and the wife refuses to give complete answers. You can also take five minutes where you both talk and no one listens. This should jar your old way of doing things out of its rut. The discomfort created by the change will bring you laughter. Encourage each other to stay loose and remember to keep doing it over time until it's no longer a big problem.

In today's time-conscious world, you don't need to delay your fun because you don't have time. For couples, play can be short and uncomplicated. It just needs to be fun. Here are a few more examples of playing with the issues. If one partner has trouble making decisions, create a playful list of twenty silly, unthreatening decisions he or she can make and then be sure to use them. When stuck on an issue, create a fun verbal phrase to work on it. To deal with tense, angry situations, for example, you might say, "God's not willing and the creeks are rising." Use anything that will work for you as a couple. The more you practice, the easier it will get. Keep on telling yourselves that fun is a good thing. *Fun is a good thing* is a great daily mantra. You can chant it together each morning. Laughter and play will help you live together with tolerance, forgiveness, and change.

Patterns can be a heavy-duty issue to work with as you may have realized by now. However, you do not always have to be serious in dealing with them. As you sort your patterns out, lighten things up a bit. In the course of working on patterns, you could pretend you both climbed the mountain of life to consult the Relationship Guru about the secret of happy relationships. When you reach the top and you find the Guru, you ask the question, "Master, what creates a happy relationship?" The master replies, "It ain't how deep you fish, it's how you wiggle the worm." You, of course, are left to ponder the deeper meaning together. Deciding on different kinds of common wisdom for the Guru to impart is a great way to inject levity into serious things.

Meanwhile, pondering the master's reply may also help you realize that one of the problems in keeping your relationship healthy may be resistance to working on your relationship. People frequently believe they should not have to do so. Why they don't is something of a mystery. However, if you are wondering when the work stops in a relationship, the answer is never. It is a good idea to work at loving each other on a daily basis. Loving work can be very pleasurable once we feel and see the results. There is an old Christian hymn that admonishes us to "Work Till Jesus Comes." This should be the credo of every relationship no matter what your spiritual beliefs.

While it does seem ironic that you have to work at loving one another, it is wonderful that it does not have to be a pain. You worked in the beginning of your relationship to make your partner love you, and it was fun because your motivation was stronger. If you want to keep laughing and loving each other for a lifetime, you need to make and keep your relationship your first priority. Try to follow the advice of Franklin Roosevelt: "When you get to the end of your rope, tie a knot in it and hold on." While you're "hanging in there," find a way to regain your laughter, and love will be there too.

All the hurts of childhood were serious when you were a child, and you stored them away because you needed to cope at the time. However, once you achieved the exalted status of adulthood, these issues were no longer serious. Therefore, when you can identify them, or even stumble into them, you can play with them together. You no longer have to struggle so hard. If you can relax and have fun while coping with your issues, your relationship will be happier, and it will last. Instead of thinking about new dance partners for life, you will find you want to keep dancing with "the one who brung you" because your partner is the one with whom you really share life's rhythm.

Exercise

Laughter Affirmation for Couples

It's important to keep your minds consciously and unconsciously seeking laughter and fun in your relationship on a long-term basis. The following exercise will tap into your unconscious minds and create a blueprint for fun that your minds will follow and begin to implement on a regular basis.

First, set aside time each day to do this together. It doesn't take more than five minutes. Hold hands, close your eyes, and imagine yourselves enveloped by a colored cloud of mist. The color should be the color of laughter and fun to you. Breathe the colored mist into your lungs and repeat the following affirmation. (You can peep at the words if you need to.)

We are magnets to fun and laughter.
We create fun and laughter now and forever.
Our lives are fun, and we allow it to be easy.

After repeating the affirmation once, exhale the mist. Inhale again and repeat. Do it a total of three times at least once a day. You will find that fun and laughter start to take place more effortlessly than ever before. Your mind will create it for you even when you are occupied with other thoughts and concerns.

Among those whom I like,
I can find no common denominator,
but among those whom I love,
I can: all of them make me laugh.
—W.H. Auden

Chapter 4

Talking, Talking Happy Talk

Well, I don't think much of giving advice...
but I'll say this much—what's worked for us
is to keep a good, healthy sense of humor
and not take marriage or each other too seriously.
—Lucy VanDenburg

The setting is a South Pacific paradise. As your eyes devour the lush backdrop of a green, tropical island floating in a clear, blue ocean, you suddenly hear a beautiful voice singing about "happy talk." The song lifts you up and lingers in your mind. "Talking, talking happy talk," she sings. "Talk about things you like to do." With her heart reflected in her voice, Bloody Mary sings her wisdom to young lovers in the movie, *South Pacific*. It is a wonderful song and great advice, but most of us would not find it necessary. In the beginning of our relationships, the magic of love weaves a verbal spell, and we are generally full of things to say and eager to listen to our partners. Everything they say seems interesting and important. We literally hang on their every word and marvel at their wisdom. Everything is "happy talk."

Most of us intend to reside in this land of verbal

enchantment forever. Alas, as time passes, the spell wears thin, and we seem to lose interest in each other. We awake from our deep sleep, not to find our "prince or princess charming" but a stranger who speaks a language we barely understand and with whom we can no longer communicate. We become confused, and it's hard to know what to do. Fortunately, we do have choices. We can cultivate our laughter and playfully work toward learning to communicate again, or we can accept living with someone we don't understand which is not a happy prospect. We can, however, live with "happy talk" in our relationships if we choose to do so.

What Happens to the Happy Talk?

A sense of humor is one thing
no one will admit to not having.
—Mark Twain

What happens to the happy talk? was a question that concerned Susan and Larry. They were a couple that had lost not only the happy talk in their relationship but almost any talk at all. When they first met, they found lots to talk about, even though they moved in radically different professional worlds—she a school teacher, he a stockbroker. Their supply of topics seemed inexhaustible. They talked about world affairs and business, of course, but they also shared their dreams, their needs, and significant events in their lives. Susan and Larry also talked of love. They called each other often and regularly talked late into the night. As well as significant conversation, loving, verbal nonsense seemed perfectly normal and somehow terribly important. Cupid's arrow had filled them with things to say and had given them the eloquence to say them. They were in a fever of communication that they never dreamed would end.

The fever finally broke, however, and they awoke one day to find themselves sitting across the breakfast table from one another with nothing to say. Their minds seemed wiped clean of interesting ideas. The fuel which had once propelled their conversations now seemed to run "information wipers" in their minds. They felt bored with one another and experienced a kind of panic about whether or not they would ever really want to talk again. Despair overtook them as they wondered if this were all there would ever be. Larry, a man with a wry sense of humor, thought to himself as he stared across at Susan that he hadn't known that when the "cat gets your tongue," it also gets your thoughts as well. He figured there must be many smart, talkative cats out there in the world with extra tongues and thoughts. He also wondered what in the world he and Susan could do about the situation.

Many couples find themselves in this place, and they don't know why. This ultimate failure to communicate is an interesting paradox. If the cultural wisdom that men and women communicate differently is true, why are they able to bridge the differences at first? Somehow, love and the wild excitement that goes with it spill over into the arena of communication. Initially, men and women communicate openly and enjoy talking with one another. Although differences exist, they are not a problem.

Long-term commitment seems to be the culprit that interferes with communication. Somehow, it trips a booby trap of boredom, disinterest, and repetitive behaviors. When we decide to stay together forever, it's as if we shed the exhilaration of love to emerge in a plodding, responsible, predictable coexistence with nothing much to say. Our culture teaches us to expect that dull existence after commitment. We are repeatedly exposed to variations on the stereotype of the man sitting silently in front of the TV, drinking a beer, and gripping the remote control in self-defense while his partner yaps in the background as she makes her frazzled way through her mundane life.

Paradoxically, we whirl through our love affairs transported by endorphins and adrenalin. Romance directs us to marriage, the pinnacle of romantic love and communication. Then after marriage, another image takes over. Culturally, we see marriage as "the old ball and chain" for men and "women's work is never done" for women. Our communication becomes little more than complaining, both internally and externally. Even our humor accentuates the negative differences between husbands and wives. Many marital quotes by the famous also accentuate the idea that men and women are trapped in their relationships. According to Oscar Wilde, for example, " The one charm of marriage is that it makes a life of deception absolutely necessary for both parties."

If we were to diagram the process as it is, it might look like this.

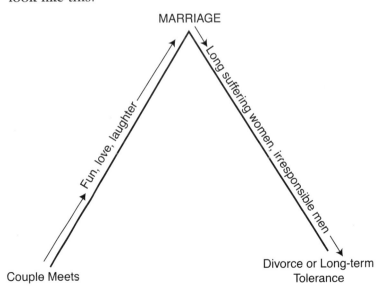

Why not work toward a diagram like this instead?

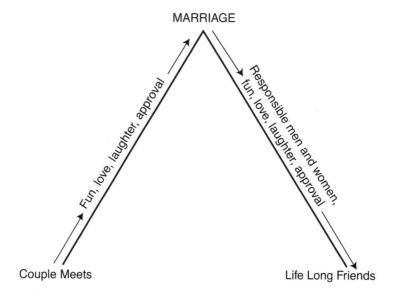

MARRIAGE

Fun, love, laughter, approval

Responsible men and women, fun, love, laughter, approval

Couple Meets

Life Long Friends

The second diagram is currently prevented from becoming reality by partners focusing on their own emotional needs and becoming less interested in what the other person has to say. After commitment, conversation does continue about the day-to-day details of the relationship and the family, but these discussions are often stressful, tedious, or critical. As partners become less a priority for each other, they begin to feel less cared about and understood. Yard work, cooking, clothes washing, grocery shopping, and other details of life supplant that high-flying feeling of being special and number one in importance. The loss of feeling special seeps into the relationship slowly, and partners instinctively react with resentment. They distance from each other without fully knowing why.

As the distance between them develops, many partners subsequently use negative humor about their relationships in their attempt to cope with their pain and confusion. Such humor is common in our society and readily accessible to couples. For example, one cartoon shows a woman shooting her husband in the arm. Irritated, he looks at her and says, "Did you do that to be hurtful?" This sort of humor may help us cope, but it doesn't help us feel better about one another because it reflects our resentment, not our love.

This resentment between partners grows from feeling taken for granted and unappreciated. It's realistic to expect to be more important to one's partner than the mortgage payment or the washer and dryer. People do not begin their futures together seeing themselves as the least important things in their partner's lives. We don't form relationships so we can heave a sigh of relief that the good times are now over. However, as we settle into our relationships, we do allow the good times to end. We focus on the responsibilities of everyday life and neglect to nourish our relationships with laughter and fun—we forget to talk "happy talk."

As we put aside fun and laughter, issues like the need for attention, approval or acceptance get stirred up, and we begin focusing on the things our partner neglects doing or neglects doing right. We also begin to talk about those faults and, not surprisingly, no one enjoys hearing about his or her faults. In fact, according to François, Duc de la Rochefoucauld, "We only confess our little faults to persuade people that we have no large ones." If our larger faults are a point of focus with our partners, we often stop talking.

To explain this negative form of communication, we need to cock our ears toward the past where we will hear our mothers and fathers pointing out our duties, our responsibilities, and our inadequacies. Caught up in old feelings we don't understand, we allow our adoration and unqualified approval of our partners to sink beneath the waves of a committed relationship. As adoration sinks and commitment allows old issues to rise, communication patterns connected to childhood survival also float to the surface. We tend to cling to them desperately and without thought or consideration because without these ways of communicating, we fear we will drown.

Our fear for our survival feels very serious, and we can lose our sense of humor over it if we're not careful. If, however, we nourish our laughter and our sense of the absurd, we don't have to "go down with the ship." We can learn new ways of communicating which will allow us to continue to talk with our partners with interest and love.

Communication Is Learned

If I can get you to laugh with me, you like me better, which makes you more open to my ideas.
—John Cleese

One of the major roadblocks to new, effective communication with our partners is our tendency to blame our failure to communicate on biology. Certainly, men and women have biological differences, but communication is not one of them. Communication is a learned skill, and unfortunately, boys and girls who are born with the same abilities to feel and process emotions learn to communicate differently. This difference makes it difficult for us to understand one another later on. We could teach communication skills that would move the sexes closer together but, for some reason, we stubbornly continue to send men and women down very different verbal paths.

We teach men, for example, to speak directly and literally, sticking to what is tangible. Culturally, they learn to explore things that don't require the discussion of feelings. Therefore, on one level they can talk about things like technology, history, scientific theory, and politics or, on a more concrete level that is always safe, they may discuss sports, business, and cars. It is rarely acceptable for a man to discuss feelings, and that lack of acceptance forces him to struggle with his feelings alone. Men often find refuge in humor because it helps them cope and offers some expression of their pent-up feelings. They are more comfortable using humor than laughter because humor is safely intellectual. Men often curb their laughter because it requires a loss of control and the release of feelings.

If, however, a man does decide to talk about his feelings, he usually seeks out a woman. In fact, this masculine need for verbal intimacy can be one of the original foundations of a relationship. Ironically, our culture subsequently snatches away this need for communication as Lucy snatches the football from Charlie Brown in the Peanuts cartoon series. After commitment, our culture dictates that a man begin to relate to his partner according to a blueprint that eliminates intimate talk.

Women, too, have the football snatched away at the last minute. The talking and sharing they loved in the beginning of their relationship dribbles away with the awesome responsibilities of a formal, long-term relationship. Not realizing they also play a part in the demise of good communication, women wonder in true puzzlement why their male partners no longer talk with them.

A woman's part in the loss of communication is the training women receive to "talk indirectly." Too much candor is considered unfeminine and may be perceived as threatening by those they love. Such a threat might interfere with a woman's nurturing responsibilities in a relationship or a family. Consequently, women learn multiple ways to ease around a point in order to avoid upsetting other people. They rarely have any idea how unclear they may be to their listener. One man learned to work with his partner's vague communication style by playfully easing her to her point by smiling and saying, "Could you please beat around the bush a little closer to the point?"

Still, direct or indirect, society allows women to talk about feelings, and they do so regularly. Women also maintain more spontaneous laughter than men do because it is okay for them to lose control and express feelings. Unfortunately, because women are generally indirect, they often receive unsatisfactory responses from their male partners who don't understand their thoughts or feelings and have no idea how to respond. In addition, further complicating matters, men and women don't appreciate the differences in the communication styles of the sexes. Instead of enjoying and utilizing what each has to offer, they focus on the differences as reasons to disapprove of each other.

For example, men stereotypically see women as emotional, flighty, nagging, and confusing. Women see men as self-absorbed, distant, withholding, and sex-crazed. Neither stereotype is true and only serves to feed a dysfunctional lack of communication that evolves downhill. Unfortunately, this downhill evolution includes bountiful jokes about male and female differences and, although people laugh, this ongoing ridicule of one another only hurts our struggle to communicate. Laughter and humor need to be positive in order to help us talk to one another.

In the beginning, before locking into the stereotypes, our relationships are upbeat, complimentary, and born of the overwhelming need to be with another person who loves us as we are. Senses of humor reign, and we truly delight in each other's laughter. Imagine how wonderful the world would be if men and women retained approval of each other and liked the other sex as much as they like their own. We would be irresistible to one another for life, and how we could talk! If we maintained a positive view of the loving need to share our thoughts and feelings, our original attraction for each other could live on in our relationships. Instead of love dying young in an impulsive act of passion like the love of Romeo and Juliet, love could die old and emotionally rich with Romeo and Juliet tottering into bed together with a tender hug and kiss of life-long intimacy.

The Dilemma of Expression—
Thoughts or Feelings?

Humor is laughing at what you
haven't got when you ought to have it.
—Langston Hughes

To explore the dilemma of expression, we need to revisit Susan and Larry back at the breakfast table where they found each other to be emotional strangers. At this point, we can begin to see why they were caught in a quagmire of misunderstanding. They faced each other daily with lots of feelings on both sides and absolutely no idea how to express them to each other. No one taught them how to talk to each other after the new in the relationship wore off.

One reason couples like Susan and Larry don't talk is that feelings are not very acceptable socially. Feelings can create controversy and unrest and are therefore discouraged. Because of this unspoken social guideline, men and women learn to suppress their true feelings at an early age and talk about what they think instead of what they feel. Thoughts are more controllable and less intense than feelings and are therefore more acceptable. However, people confusingly describe their thoughts as "feelings" in conversations. For example, a person might say, "I don't feel like you listen to me." He or she is really saying, "I think you don't listen." The unspoken feeling underlying the hurt of not being heard might be irritation, for example. Since the feeling is not expressed, the communication in this case is vague and misguiding. Thoughts expressed as feelings add to the confusion we all have about communication.

Labeling our thoughts as feelings confuses us because real feelings take place spontaneously and before our thoughts. Feelings relate specifically to what happens to us. Thoughts are our interpreted and edited version of our feelings and may or may not be accurate. As a result, when we only share our thoughts, we may not communicate what we really feel or need to say. Then, new feelings occur which we translate into thoughts that create new feelings and so on. Unless we are clear about what we feel and what we think, we communicate poorly, and we may wind up without communication at all. This was certainly true for Susan and Larry.

Susan might say to Larry, for example, "I feel you don't love me anymore."

Larry, who does care, says, "But I do love you."

Susan responds, "You never tell me."

Larry, feeling frustrated, says, "I told you yesterday."

Susan says, "But you haven't told me today."

Larry, exasperated and feeling helpless, says, "Okay, I love you."

Susan, still unsatisfied, replies, "It's not the same when I have to ask you."

Poor Larry doesn't have a chance. He's caught in Susan's frozen childhood need to be loved, and nothing he says will be good enough. A playful approach at the end where he says, "I love you, I love you, I love you" may be helpful because it reassures her without attempting to be logical. Frozen needs are not logical, and attempts to meet them logically are doomed to failure. We can laugh about them, however, if neither person is stuck in the intensity of the feeling. Larry would be ill-advised to laugh about Susan's frozen need, for example, unless she can laugh about it and invites him to laugh with her.

When she was a child, Susan might have sought reassurance for her need for love by picking a daisy and asking it the answer by plucking its petals one by one and saying, "He loves me; he loves me not." If she got the wrong answer, she could start over with a new daisy and repeat the process until it came out right. The child's solution would have been simple and direct and depended only on her own ingenuity. The adult Susan pursued reassurance indirectly from the man himself and depended on his ingenuity. As Susan plucked the petals with Larry, the answers varied from petal to petal, driving her crazy. At the end of it all, Susan angrily held a daisy with no petals and couldn't start over because Larry had nothing left to pluck.

Susan and Larry were trapped in a spider web of poor communication. The web was an intricate, dysfunctional pattern of inadequate communication skills learned in childhood and the unconscious stimulation of unsatisfied needs. Susan was really asking Larry to love her and let her know it regularly. However, she did it indirectly, and Larry felt manipulated, criticized, and defensive. He finally told her he loved her because he felt he had no choice. Naturally, he felt resentful. Susan then rejected his grudging declaration of love as not good enough which frustrated him even more. At the end of the conversation, Susan still felt unloved and unhappy because the feelings created by the poor communication prevented her from feeling the love Larry actually had for her. Larry was angry that she didn't just know he loved her. He married her, didn't he? The dialogue between them served no purpose other than to add to the frustration and resentment building in them both.

Because they wanted the daisy's last petal to be "He or she loves me," they kept trying to improve their relationship so they could talk, laugh, and have fun again. Finally, at their wit's end, Susan and Larry attended a marital workshop on laughter in relationships. With other couples, they explored the problems of their communi-

cation from a laughter perspective. They learned that
although talking together is important, it doesn't always
have to be serious. Serious issues can be approached
with a playful mindset that allows people to laugh and
lighten up while they work things out. Supporting that
idea, Susan and Larry learned playful communication
techniques and tools that helped them lighten up their
communication. Play is the primary key to laughter, and
adults need to use play to understand and deal with serious things just as children do.

Playful Ways to Communicate

Humor is often a way of communicating that allows
things to be said that couldn't be said otherwise.
—Ralph Nader

One technique Susan and Larry practiced was creating several different playful ways to say, "I love you" that
actually communicated love in a satisfying and unthreatening way. For example, they used different voices to say
"I love you" like a high, falsetto voice, a deep voice with
a foreign accent, and the voice of Donald Duck. They
said, "I love you" in foreign languages. They wrote it on
unexpected places like the toilet seat lid and the milk car-
ton. Their spontaneous play with the expression of love
eliminated the serious, score-keeping issue for them.

Another way Susan and Larry began to crack the
silence that had developed between them was to create a
list of the things about each other that were irritating.
Under each item, they concocted a light, fun way to deal
with it. They found during the exercise that the more
serious the items were for each of them, the harder it was
to develop a light way to cope. However, with a little help

from other couples at the workshop, they persevered and found a way. In addition to lightening up their communication, the exercise opened opportunities for straightforward discussion about the issues as well. The playfulness and the search for positive solutions made it safe for them to talk on a deeper level.

One of the complaints Susan put on her list about Larry was his annoying tendency to talk to her as if she was less knowledgeable than he. Her playful solution was to sit at his feet, look into his face with rapt attention and awe, and compliment his teaching skills. As she became the exaggerated student, he became the exaggerated teacher, and they began to play. Although the behavior did not disappear, it no longer shut them down, and they could talk about it.

One of Larry's complaints about Susan was her need to control their spending. His playful solution was to hold up a sign that said "Hopelessly poor. Need money. God bless you." This wry bit of humor helped them gain some perspective and the desire to do things a little differently for each other. Susan saw more clearly how Larry felt when she was so controlling about the money, and she began to work on being less controlling.

The lack of seriousness in the solutions actually made the issues less difficult to talk about because they seemed smaller somehow. They could see some of their more irritating behaviors without feeling that the behaviors made them bad people. Susan and Larry learned to see behavior as what they "do," not who they are. They also took heart from the idea that what they learned, they could unlearn. Because of the laughter their new skills created and the greater ease of communication that went with it, they found they still had lots to talk about and that they could do it in a way that was satisfying to them both. Their mutual understanding began to deepen as their communication improved.

The exercise Susan and Larry used to unlock their

inability to communicate works for many people because it pops couples loose from their rigid, serious perceptions of one another's behavior. The following is a sample list of some of the irritating behaviors and the playful solutions that the couples at Susan and Larry's workshop developed. Perhaps you will recognize you and your partner in the list of behaviors, or you will be inspired to create your own list. Hopefully, the playful solutions created by the couples at the workshop will trigger some playful solutions of your own.

Behavior: Woman pushes to get all the chores done on her time schedule.
Solution: Man goes on an exaggerated twelve-hour marathon of chore accomplishment insisting his partner go along with him. Just thinking about the marathon made his partner feel less pushy, and she could feel herself back off. This immediate response made them both laugh.

Behavior: Man sits glued to the TV refusing to communicate with his partner.
Solution: Woman adopts a tiny TV as her pet. She carries it with her everywhere and is always absorbed in it. It slowly dawns on her partner that she is not available to him, and he can't communicate with her. Watching TV becomes unimportant as he focuses on making his partner talk to him. The irony of the role reversal eventually strikes home. They laugh together as they realize how absurd behavior can be.

Behavior: Man continually forgets to lower the toilet seat and his partner often plops her rear in the water when she goes to the bathroom in the dark.
Solution: Woman surprises her partner by dunking his genitals in a glass of cold water in the middle of the night. A play fight ensues when he carries her to

the toilet and dunks her bottom. She splashes him with water, and they have such fun, they decide to make love.

Behavior: Woman constantly points out how messy her partner is.
Solution: Man refuses to shave, bathe, or pick up anything at all. He leaves much more clutter than usual and uses atrocious table manners. He acknowledges his messiness to his partner with a great deal of regret. He attributes it to brain damage caused by a caretaking mother. He begs his partner to help him find help for his "messy" disorder. She gets the point as his silliness delights her, and they laugh.

Behavior: Woman complains constantly that her partner doesn't do his fair share.
Solution: Man goes on a complete strike. He no longer does what he has been doing and goes out of his way to be unfair. He does give her a diamond ring for being so long-suffering and promises a big gift once a year if she will continue working harder than he does. Woman sees that her partner does more than she thought and is trying to be helpful. She decides to reject the suffering role and the gifts in favor of some help. Both partners giving a loud thank you after help is received creates laughter and appreciation.

Behavior: Man spends large sums of money without consulting his partner.
Solution: Woman talks constantly, 24 hours a day, about the large purchase she's planning to make. She does not consult her partner nor ask his opinion or permission. She simply plans aloud. The more she plans, the clearer her point becomes. Finally, he begs her to stop planning aloud. He promises to consult

with her in the future. She lets out one more tiny plan as a teaser, and they laugh.

It's important for couples to realize that these light solutions to irritating behaviors don't necessarily stop the behaviors. They do offer a different perspective to both partners and, as they approach the issues less seriously, partners can talk about them and work toward solutions that will work on a long-term basis. If they stay serious, partners will more than likely stay locked in the behaviors unable to express the feelings that go with them. Playfulness opens up good communication, and good communication leads to fewer problems between partners.

Criticism Ain't No Way to Communicate Feelings

Humor is the healthy way of feeling a
"distance" between one's self and the problem,
a way of standing off
and looking at one's problem with perspective.
—Rollo May

If play creates laughter and laughter contributes to good communication, what prevents couples from keeping fun and laughter a priority? The main reason is the failure of most couples to see the need to focus on fun. They mistakenly believe it should happen by itself. However, realistically, to have fun we must create it. If we make no regular effort to have fun, serious things will interfere to the point of blocking the laughter, fun, and good communication that could be there.

Criticism is one example of serious things that prevent good communication. Criticism creates worry in people about being a "bad" person in the eyes of others. This particular worry is so common in our society it should be considered a major cultural phenomenon. It certainly creates major issues of communication for people in relationships. For example, our worry about being "bad" causes us to be defensive. We then criticize our partner in an attempt to feel better about ourselves. He or she reacts defensively and does the same thing to us. Then, we are caught in a negative cycle of disapproval and unhappiness.

Factually speaking, no one appreciates criticism of any kind. Seldom do you hear someone seriously say, "Thank you so much for criticizing me." It just doesn't feel good. If things are not particularly tense, however, couples can begin playing with the problem by deliberately looking at each other with a big smile and saying "Thank you so much for the criticism." The incongruence of this playful technique can take the sting out of the criticism itself, and change becomes more of a possibility.

The irony of criticism in relationships is that it is born of our instinctive drive to feel better about ourselves. We criticize our partners for not doing all it takes to make us feel good. In so doing, we can reopen each other's old hurts from the past such as feeling like a "bad" boy or girl. If we do so, we will also reawaken the communication patterns we developed to cope with the hurt. We will then say and do things in the present that we might consider amazing if we weren't the ones saying and doing them. For example:

- We retreat into silence.
- We jabber.
- We talk all around the issues.
- We agree whether we mean it or not.
- We talk in monosyllables like yep and nope.
- We drop hints.
- We plead.

* We criticize.
* We yell.
* We deliver guilt trips.
* We don't listen.
* We interrupt.
* We whine.
* We leave.

The ironic thing about all this ineffective communication is that underneath it all is a yearning to express ourselves in a way that allows others to know and understand us. Instead, in our need to protect ourselves, we create less understanding. We become so lost as to the real meaning of what we say and hear that we are truly "so confused we don't know if we've lost a horse or found a rope." Then, we are not sure we want to stay together. At this point, most people are not laughing. They are serious, and the seriousness causes them to remain in the problem. When we are too serious about something, we lose perspective and are blind to our options for change.

Ken and Bailey, for example, had been married a very long time. They had weathered a great many painful things together but had never really been able to talk about them. They muddled along feeling dissatisfied and unhappy, and each criticized the other for the state of their relationship. Finally, their unhappiness built to such a point they found themselves considering divorce. After discussing their alternatives, they decided to seek counseling instead. They wanted to save the friendship they knew was there beneath all the misunderstandings. They chose a form of counseling which utilized laughter in the healing process because they like to laugh, and they had not been able to laugh together for a long time.

As a result of beginning counseling, Ken and Bailey came face to face with two things. One, they realized they wanted to stay together. Two, they found they were unable to identify most of their feelings, much less talk about them. As they reflected on their many years of criticism, they found this ignorance of their feelings somewhat astonishing. They could identify some of their problems, of course, so that is where they began to try to communicate.

Like Kathy and Chris in chapter one, they found that if they gave their issues comical names, they were less threatening to talk about. For example, they named the emotional distance between them "The Gulf." Their arguments about not spending enough time together were "The Gulf War." By using this simple tool, they were able to loosen things up a bit, so they could at least try to resolve some of the serious things they had hoarded feelings about over the years.

In addition to adopting comical names for some of their issues, Ken and Bailey also devised a way to work on identifying and expressing their feelings. After developing a list of feeling terms like irritation, frustration, worry, caring, and love, they spent at least a half hour a week in conversations heavily sprinkled with feeling terms. Sometimes the conversations were about real and serious things going on in their lives, and sometimes they were about silly, fictional things. The exercise became a real game for them, and they had such fun, they were somewhat surprised to realize they had become aware of many of their feelings. It was also no longer a form of purgatory to express them. Ken and Bailey had discovered a universal truth. When couples allow important things to be less serious by using laughter in their relationship, it eases or eliminates the shutdown in communication caused by anxiety, fear, and anger.

Like Ken and Bailey, most of us have trouble identifying our feelings. We think in terms of "end results" like upset, stressed out, bothered, or overwhelmed and consider them feelings. This way of thinking prevents us from focusing on the feelings that cause the results. To assist you in identifying feelings, a number of feeling terms have been listed below. You may want to check out your "feeling awareness" and see how well you can identify your own feelings. You can do this by listing all the feelings you have in a single day on paper. If you have a long list, your awareness is good. If your list is particularly short, you may want to work on developing your awareness.

After you do this stretching exercise for your feelings, you and your partner can try the exercise that worked for Ken and Bailey and see if it enhances the knowledge you have of your mutual feelings. If you develop a greater feeling awareness in your relationship, it will help you talk with one another about your issues. To get you started on the exercise, a sample of one of Ken and Bailey's good-humored, feeling-oriented conversations is included below the list of feeling terms.

Feeling Words

Confused	Guilty
Angry	Frustrated
Embarrassed	Frightened
Ashamed	Depressed
Jealous	Anxious
Confident	Happy
Hopeful	Love
Caring	Generous
Tender	Nurturing
Worried	Irritated

Sample Playful Conversation
(The feeling words are underlined.)

"When we went to dinner at The Green Pea, I felt confused by the menu. I couldn't tell if I would get a baked potato or not. I felt embarrassed asking the waiter."

"Well, I felt a little <u>guilty</u> not anticipating that problem for you. I was <u>ashamed</u> of myself as a man. I should have been able to protect you from that confusing menu."

"It's very <u>loving</u> and <u>generous</u> of you to feel so strongly about my <u>embarrassment</u>. I felt a little <u>anxious</u> before I got my meal, but when the baked potato came with everything on it, it boosted my <u>confidence</u>, and I felt very <u>happy</u>."

" We must remember this in the future when we go out to eat. We will only pick restaurants where we feel <u>confident</u> we can handle the menu and where we can find the restrooms without asking. It's <u>embarrassing</u> to have to ask and <u>frustrating</u> and <u>depressing</u> if we have to go to the restroom and can't find it on our own. Eating out should never be <u>anxiety-producing</u> or <u>confusing</u>. I will take better care of things in the future so you can rest assured that you will be able to eat with <u>confidence</u>. Dining out will no longer have to <u>worry</u> or <u>depress</u> you."

"You are my <u>loving</u>, <u>caring</u>, protective knight in shining armor, and I thank you. I feel so <u>happy</u> I think I'll do a little cheer: 'Two bits, four bits, six bits, a dollar. I feel so <u>loved</u>, I'll smile big and holler! Yeah!'"

The Importance of Listening

Humor puts things in perspective
and helps us to see things inside out and upside down.
Humor requires thought and a strong degree of compassion.
—Jerry and Helen Weiss

In addition to the walls partners build of unspoken feelings, many couples have difficulty communicating because they no longer listen to one another. Listening is the skill of greatest importance in communication.

Almost everyone has a real need to be listened to because
so very few of us had parents who listened carefully e-
nough when we were children. As a result, we grew up
interrupting others so we would get a chance to talk, talking a mile a minute in order to finish before we were
interrupted, repeating ourselves over and over in the
hope that we would finally be acknowledged, or listening
only long enough to plan our next statement. In our
need to be heard, we lost the art of listening.

Listening is a monumental issue for people and a skill
which most of us really have to struggle to master.
Interestingly, our laughter is an important part of listening because it relieves the anxiety that shuts down our
ability to really hear other people. If we stop laughing
together, it compounds our problems in listening to one
another. However, laughter or no laughter, we hear men
and women consistently complaining to anyone who will
listen that their partner doesn't listen to them. They complain because a partner who doesn't listen causes them
to feel invalidated and unimportant. These uncomfortable feelings then lead couples into arguments where
negative feelings build on one another. Such arguments
are all the result of the difficulty in knowing how to listen.

Therefore, in light of the fact that we don't know how
to listen to each other, it is ironic that many arguments
take place over what was or was not said as each individual remembers it. People repeat what they believe they
said or what they believe they heard with great vigor. Few
people will admit they may not have heard the other person correctly. Instead of learning to listen, we defend our
lack of listening skills without even realizing it. We seem
to think we are born listeners with no need to learn. This
is the communication equivalent of claiming we are born
knowing how to drive, and, just as in driving, skills often
take second place to the need to be right. It is important
to note that people who hang on to their ability to laugh
at their own inconsistencies in their communication with

their partners make better learners, listeners, and probably better drivers.

Our need to be right is such a common problem that humor pops up to help us cope with it. A T-Shirt in a Colorado resort asks, "If a man speaks in the woods without a woman around, will he still be wrong?" Nancy Astor, a British politician, once quipped, "The first time Adam had a chance he laid the blame on a woman."

We can see that both men and women have a powerful need to be right. As a result, when the real issue in an argument is lost in the surface issue of right and wrong, partners instinctively drop into emotionally defensive postures and prowl around the argument verbally for hours, days, or weeks. As they heatedly defend what they said or didn't say, heard or didn't hear, feelings are hurt and resentment builds. The issues are confused, and partners mill around them like emotional cattle, bawling out their pain with no clear idea where it came from. While the bawling goes on, there is no communication. There is only noise that is meaningless to both people. An American Indian proverb sums it up nicely. It reminds us to "Listen or thy tongue will keep thee deaf." (And dumb.)

To avoid such arguments and unnecessary pain, strengthening our listening skills is essential. Really listening to each other allows us to hear and acknowledge one another, which meets a basic need in us all. While listening of any kind is good, focused listening is even better. It is a skill all couples would do well to cultivate. It insures that one person really listens while the other talks. The following exercise will help you develop focused listening skills. The rules for the exercise are simple:

1. Decide on a speaker and a listener.
2. The speaker chooses a topic and begins talking.
3. The listener may not interrupt or comment on topic content.
4. The listener may ask for clarification, but that is all.

The listener's job is to listen only.
5. After the speaker finishes, switch roles. Partners need to take turns learning to listen because it is important and creates good feelings in both partners.

After each of you has listened to the other, notice the difficulty and the feelings you had while listening only. Share the feelings with each other. Discuss the problems you feel may have stemmed from not listening to each other.

Interestingly, when listening occurs, there are fewer arguments between partners because there are fewer misunderstandings. A pleasant, nonthreatening way to practice listening is to make up comical, or otherwise entertaining little stories. Practicing listening doesn't have to be a drag. One person gets to talk and create, and the other gets to listen to a good story. If you are afraid you can't make up a good story, don't worry. Any kind of story or tale of events will do. If you want to go a more serious route, another way to begin practicing listening is to tell each other your life stories. Very few people in relationships have heard their partner's complete life story. It's a good story to know so listen carefully.

Resistance to Change

A good sense of humor helps to overlook the unbecoming, understand the unconventional, tolerate the unpleasant, overcome the unexpected, and outlast the unbearable.
—Anonymous

Most couples really do want to be better listeners. They want to communicate. They repeatedly express this desire to each other, their friends, and their counselors. It is so important to couples that, because of this, magazines frequently sell themselves by headlines promising such things as "Seven Steps to Communicate Your Way Out of the Doghouse" or "Five Ways to Get a Man to Listen to You Without Having to Wear a G-String." Television talk shows also take advantage of our desire to communicate and show millions of viewers the worst and the best in couples communication. People watch couples humiliate each other by yelling at each other and viciously criticizing each other on the air, and then, just as eagerly watch them get married while vowing eternal love hanging from a hot air balloon. The need for communication causes us to crave even ridiculous information on how to talk to one another.

In addition to buying that information in magazines and watching it on television shows, couples also read lots of books on love and communication. They get fact after fact on how to talk to each other but, still, communication suffers. Couples want to change for the better but resist it at the same time. Seeking change is somewhat like a baby wearing a dirty diaper. It makes us uncomfortable on one level, but there is simultaneously a warm sort of comfort in what we have so we hate to give it up. Change makes us ambivalent.

Spencer and Calley are a good example of a couple who wanted to change their communication but found it hard to give up the comfort of what they already had, no matter how dysfunctional it was. They both talked a lot, and neither one listened. As a result, they had many misunderstandings. Like many people, they each listened only long enough to frame their next comment. Neither understood the other as a person even though they had been together several years. They both talked so much and with such anxiety about their own feelings, they had no opportunity to even try to understand the other's feelings. They had a "super duper" failure to communicate.

Despite their difficulties, both Spencer and Calley did try to express their needs to each other, but because of their difficulty listening and their different communication styles, they failed miserably. Spencer, for example, tended to announce that he was depressed, overwhelmed, tired, or bored and expected Calley to know exactly what he needed to feel better. Whether he needed time alone, nurturance, praise, or some kind of assistance, he thought she should know what he needed and give it to him. She felt totally frustrated that she had to guess what he needed, and most of the time, she guessed wrong. She felt like a candidate on the TV quiz show "Jeopardy" who could never get out of the minus column.

Calley, however, did no better than Spencer in expressing her needs. Like Spencer, she also expressed her needs indirectly, but instead of announcing her mood, she listed her obligations and chores for the day aloud and complained about feeling overwhelmed or cried because she felt ignored and unloved. Spencer never clearly understood that she needed help and acknowledgement because she never specifically asked for them. Subsequently, he felt irritated by her complaining and dismissed it as whining.

Lack of good communication created the belief in both Spencer and Calley that the other person was insensitive and intolerant. Neither felt loved, accepted, or understood. Even though they could not feel the love, they continued to believe they loved each other, and that motivated them to keep trying. Trying was hard for them because they tended to allow things to move to the brink of divorce before taking action. Then, they would change things for a while, but eventually, they let themselves slip back into their old, comfortable, destructive pattern of poor communication.

Spencer and Calley were not unique in allowing things to move to the brink of divorce before they took action. Many couples do it, and some wait so long they can't pull back from the edge. They resist change until it's too late to save their relationship, and unfortunately, they slip over the edge into divorce.

The common resistance to change that couples exhibit makes little sense in light of the fact that we want our relationships to last. Although there are many theories about why resistance happens, they don't seem to help us stop the process. People continue to fight with one another in spite of the misery it creates. If one didn't know better when listening to the verbal battles raging, one would think people go out, select the meanest, dumbest, laziest, most inconsiderate person they can find, and form relationships with them.

We know this isn't true, however. Most people form relationships for good, loving reasons. However, if we do not nourish those reasons with good times and laughter, we can find ourselves using words as a lethal weapon that will wound or kill perfectly good relationships. The communication wars for couples are rooted deep in feeling. Anxiety and fear cause people to resist making changes that will help them better love and communicate with their partners. Most of us have an unrecognized fear from childhood that we aren't quite good enough as people. We depend on our partners to help us feel okay. We believe that if they really love us they will change in order to help us feel good about ourselves. Then, when they do change, we will know we are a good person, and "Voila! All's right with the world." Of course, we see no reason for us to do the same thing for our partner. We generally assume that they already know they are good enough.

Since, in reality, both partners in relationships feel the same way, neither will change very willingly. Both are waiting for the other to do it. Unfortunately, without willing change, the changes that do take place in relationships will not last. Men and women resent changing against their wills and, because of this resentment, they will revert to their old behaviors quickly even if the changes made have improved their lives and relationships.

Luckily for them, Spencer and Calley finally reached a point of wanting change badly enough that it caused them to work on their communication consistently. Utilizing a workbook full of laughter techniques, they began to try to lighten up their communication and to find entertaining ways to break up their old patterns. They began by using an exercise called "Reflect This!"

Reflect This!

Oh Lord, please fill my mouth with worthwhile stuff,
and nudge me when I've said enough.
—Anonymous

To utilize this laughter technique, Spencer and Calley chose comical topics to talk about so they weren't tempted to be stuck in their serious issues while they practiced hearing each other accurately. As one of them talked, the other would reflect what he or she said. The listener would say, "What I hear you saying is" and repeat what they heard. If it weren't correct, the talker clarified, and the listener reflected again. This continued until they were both clear about what was being said. Some of the light topics they practiced on were:

- Are there TVs in the afterlife?
- Whipped cream, silly string, and sex.
- Why "rush hour" should be called "slow hour" instead.
- The communication problems of Mickey and Minnie Mouse.

As a result of their efforts, playing with listening became fun, and "What I hear you saying is ...." became easy to remember and fun to employ. Reflecting their partner's words helped them clear up some of their misunderstandings on more important issues.

While working on their communication, Spencer and Calley also learned that words don't always mean the same things to different people. We learn different meanings in our individual families and cultures. For example, in Canada, a rubber is an eraser; in the United States, it is a contraceptive device.

Spencer and Calley also learned that in addition to different meanings, words could create different emotional impacts on people depending on how their families used them as they grew up. Tone of voice, timing, and voice inflection can change the impact of a word from one person to the next. Some examples of words with very different impacts for people are selfish, lazy, stupid, emotional, sensitive, aggressive, mature, negative, positive, and smart. To some people these are "fightin' words," and to others they are neutral or positive. There are many such words; sometimes the misunderstandings are painful, and sometimes they are hilarious. Although painful glitches in communication can be resolved with persistent patience, the more hilarity we can find in such misunderstandings, the easier it is to clarify our real meaning and resolve an issue.

Some of our most hilarious glitches in communication happen because words have different meanings in different circumstances and cause people to have complete conversations about two different things. For instance, Phil and Gloria were attending a small country church one summer evening in northern Alabama. They were standing outside talking when the choir began to sing. The crickets were also singing their own song in the dark Alabama night. Phil was listening to the crickets while Gloria listened to the choir. Suddenly, Phil said to Gloria, "You know how they make that sound, don't you? They rub their hind legs together." Gloria, startled, began to respond indignantly that they did not when she realized he wasn't talking about the choir. Then, she convulsed in laughter at the idea of the choir members rubbing their hind legs together. When she could tell Phil why she was laughing, he, too, began laughing. It was a hilarious situation that came from the different meaning words can have in different contexts.

I Love You—What Do You Mean?

Cosmic Laugh
Lifeha / deathha / joyha /sadha /
mamaha / papaha / youha / weha / theyha /
come to think of it / all is Haha.
—Anonymous

"I love you" is another, more serious example of words having different meanings to different people. Saying "I love you" can mean all is well, I love you no matter what, I like you, and so on. To Spencer "I love you" meant I'm feeling good about you, and "I love you" to Calley meant I love you no matter what. As a result, Calley was able to say "I love you" more easily than Spencer because she didn't have to feel good about him to say it. Also because of her interpretation of "I love you," Calley couldn't understand why Spencer would withhold the words she badly needed to hear, and she worried he didn't love her. Spencer, for his part, couldn't understand how she could yell at him one minute and say, "I love you" shortly thereafter. As yelling and saying "I love you" became connected for him, a positive statement became a negative one full of hidden messages and negative power.

Spencer and Calley needed to find ways to mean the same thing when they said, "I love you." They had to learn to separate their feelings from the words alone. Since yelling and saying "I love you" had created negative feelings for Spencer, they worked on yelling, "I love you" to each other. They pretended they were on opposite sides of the Grand Canyon yelling out their love. They yelled it on the phone, in the car, and around the house. They surprised each other by yelling it unexpectedly, and eventually, they were able to say it seriously, often, and without the yelling. By exaggerating a negative and playing with it, they turned it into a positive, and they were more often on the same page when they said, "I love you."

Don't Assume! You'll ASS-U-ME!?!

Nothing is quite as funny
as the unintended humor of reality.
—Steve Allen

In addition to different shades of meaning applied to various words, an additional communication problem for couples is getting just enough verbal information for them to assume the worst. Once the assumption is made, the failure to communicate is once more out of the starting gate. For example, while "four wheeling" in Colorado, Cindy and Will had a failure to communicate. Will drove the jeep off the road onto a hillside. They were both novices where jeeps were concerned and saw no danger in leaving the road. The jeep tipped, and Cindy, terrified, jumped out yelling, " The jeep's tipping over!"

Standing on the hillside below the jeep, she irrationally braced her hands against the jeep to hold it up. Will, as frightened as Cindy since the result could have been a 10,000 foot plunge to their deaths, yelled at Cindy that she didn't have to yell at him. Although the jeep did stabilize, and they were able to drive back onto the road, Will had assumed that Cindy was criticizing him for letting the jeep tip when she was just yelling a fact and a warning. Cindy's feelings were hurt when Will yelled at her for yelling at him.

Both partners were afraid in the situation, and that was the reason each said and did what they did. Assumptions, however, caused them both to get their feelings hurt at the time. Later, they were able to talk about it realistically and laugh about the fact that Cindy had ridiculously tried to hold the jeep up while Will was wedged behind the wheel. Had the jeep rolled, it would have squashed Cindy and taken Will over the cliff. Because of their assumptions at the time, they would have died with negative thoughts about each other in their minds. Dying with love in our thoughts and on our lips is our ideal, but the reality is often screaming at each other in fear. Even when we are going to die, we want it to be the other guy's fault. We want to be right to the very end.

Assumptions like those of Will and Cindy are a common problem in communication. Some couples interact constantly based on assumption and misinterpretation. They live together for a lifetime interacting like two ships that pass in the night. They see the glow of the lights, assume all is well, and sail on by. Any SOS is missed because the radar is turned off, the codes are different, or the operator is asleep at his or her station.

Thad and Peggy had just such a relationship. They loved each other, but because of problems with self-esteem, both worried the other would think they were stupid. Consequently, they frequently added assumed meanings to their partner's words rather than asking for clarification. Peggy thought for years that Thad kept her out of much of his life because he didn't trust her. In reality, Thad appeared secretive because he was afraid that if she really knew how average he was, she would find him boring. She, on the other hand, thought he was funny and intelligent, and she desperately wanted to feel closer to him. Their assumptions fed on each other until they affected the relationship negatively. The assumptions caused them both tremendous pain due to a sense of isolation and distrust.

Finally, Thad and Peggy decided with some fear and trepidation to try counseling as a last-ditch effort to create more happiness for themselves. Both were very serious about their relationship and, as a result of being too serious, had allowed laughter and fun to become low priorities. Since they had nothing to lose, however, when laughter was suggested, they decided to try it. At first, it was slow going. Their ability to lighten up and laugh was like long neglected machinery that creaks and groans with each new movement. As they cleaned, oiled, and used their laughter machinery, however, it eventually ran more easily and smoothly.

While searching for ways to play and laugh with their serious issue of assumption, they ran across a common saying that "to assume makes an ass out of you and me." (ASS-U-ME) Thad and Peggy found the saying amusing and used it to work on their problem. They began word play with all kinds of variations on the word "ass" like "ass-o-mine" instead of asinine, "ass and you shall not receive," and when they needed to know everything and be right, they considered themselves an "ass loaded with books." On a more serious note, they began to say to each other, "I assume you mean" followed by what they thought, and this allowed clarification to take place. Assumption became something they could be open about without feeling stupid. As a result, they dug out all kinds of old assumptions, many of which made them howl with laughter.

For example, Peggy remembered and confessed to

Thad that she had gotten angry with him once because she thought he had selfishly eaten all the fresh chocolate chip cookies. She felt even more aggravated because she thought he had inconsiderately left crumbs all over the table. When she alluded to it at the time and Thad had innocently responded with blank confusion, it dawned on her that her little dog had to be the culprit. He had gotten to the cookies and eaten them all. She was so embarrassed that she had blamed Thad in her mind that she had never told him. They both laughed at the image of the dog eating the cookies, getting crumbs all over, and smiling to himself when he got away with it. Now, they were able to see the humor in Peggy's ridiculous assumption that Thad would be so greedy and careless.

SPEAK UP, MY DEAR, SPEAK UP!

Part of the dearth of laughter today
is the adult fear of playing the fool.
—Dorinne Tourecamo, Family Circle, 5/27/86

In addition to making assumptions, not saying clearly what we mean, and maintaining a defensive posture, another barrier to effective communication is not speaking up when feelings occur because of your partner's behavior. People who survived childhood by trying to keep everyone happy have a major difficulty speaking up. They are always afraid of upsetting their partner and creating some kind of conflict. As a result, they keep quiet, but their feelings do not go away. Instead, the feelings slip into the unconscious mind and, over time, turn into resentment. The reasons for the resentment may blur, but the resentment itself is never very far down. It is also frequently expressed indirectly through behavior instead of verbally, head-on. An example of acting out such indirect anger would be deliberately being late for a planned activity like a dinner engagement. If you are the recipient, this kind of anger is difficult to deal with and seldom results in either person feeling any better, nor does it result in resolution of feelings.

Alanon, the spouse organization of Alcoholics Anonymous, has a saying about resentment that is not only true but also easy to remember. They tell their members that "Resentment is like peeing down your leg. You are the only one who feels it." It's their way of encouraging their members not to store useless resentment toward their spouses but to learn to express it constructively. In a relationship, if resentment is unexpressed or unresolved, it eats away at love. Resentment is unexpressed anger, and when there is enough of it, it sits astride love, joy, hope, and compassion and holds them down. It also puts the quietus on fun and laughter.

Cody was a man with a lot of resentment because he struggled with an inability to speak up in his relationship. He sought peace at all costs. Jenny, his partner, was an insecure, highly opinionated, and controlling woman. She was generally quick to express herself and quick to take offense if questioned or challenged in any way. Jenny did not see herself this way so it was hard for Cody to find a way to approach his issues with her without triggering a conflict. As a result, he grew quietly angrier and more resentful.

Cody's resentment and Jenny's prickly, insecure distrust of affection in general caused the couple to grow apart. Despite their problems, they had a strong, long-term foundation in friendship and even with the distance between them, each recognized that the loss of that friendship through divorce would be a shame. As a result, they sought help through Laughter Therapy.

Laughter Therapy was easier for Cody who was a little more playful than Jenny. She tended to be vulnerable

and serious by nature. Still, she gamely joined in as much as she could and actually found areas she could pursue lightly with some degree of comfort. In order to restore safety in their relationship, they first began to play with doing loving things for each other. Lighthearted messages left for each other in unexpected places like inside the dishwasher or on the steering wheel of the car began to thaw out the coldness created by unresolved anger. Jenny liked the notes especially and excelled at creating them. Cody was better at word play and could say funny things that expressed his love in humor that helped them laugh. The laughter and the positive, lighthearted interaction enabled them to move closer together with the boxing gloves off, and some of their serious issues became easier to discuss.

One of their serious issues was sex. Jenny and Cody had big problems in this area, and discussions were apt to be explosive and hurtful. Approaching the issue with laughter was not easy for them, but they did manage to lighten it up some. The lightness, in turn, enabled them to talk a little more openly. In talking, they discovered and shared some underlying feelings each of them had around this and other issues. Identifying their feelings helped them understand each other better and reduced their lack of communication.

Despite the fact that we generally don't think sex should be a problem, it is extremely difficult for many people to be playful about it. Therefore, it took some effort, but Jenny and Cody finally found ways to treat sex as something fun. One thing they did was creating a framework for sex with a hunting metaphor. Dressing (loosely put) in costume with hunting hats, clown noses, and nothing else helped make sex less serious. It's hard to be serious when looking at your naked partner in a hat and clown nose. As part of the game, Cody and Jenny pretended to stalk each other like the hunter after his prey. The "wounded" partner had to allow the hunter to have his way with him or her. They were creative in their game, and the hunt lent itself well to sex.

In addition to being fun, their silliness allowed better exploration of what each needed sexually because it was easier to speak up as part of the game. Then, as they knew what their partner wanted, they each put more effort toward pleasing the other. Although Jenny and Cody will probably always have to resist the pull of seriousness where sex is concerned, a continued effort to include fun in their sex life will keep things more balanced. The balance will then allow them to have discussions that are more open on the subject when needed.

As demonstrated by Jenny and Cody and the other examples in this chapter, playing with sore subjects in order to invite laughter into our relationships is important and has a positive impact on communication. It is not, however, a magic pill that will cure all our communication ills. It does allow people to be more open with each other because laughter creates safety, and issues don't seem as awesome. It allows us to express ourselves more clearly because we think more clearly when we laugh. Laughter also keeps communication fun. Couples who talk freely when they fall in love can do so forever with a little extra knowledge and added effort on their part. In order to help us keep talking with each other for a lifetime, we need to stay focused on laughing and having fun with one another. It must be a priority. Good times promote good feelings, and good feelings promote love and communication. Love that is supported by laughter can help us remember that although many things in life are important and serious, none have to be "serious" enough to shut down our communication.

Exercise

Speak to Me! Tell Me! Duh, What?

How does one learn to communicate with one's partner? Practice, practice, practice! The following exercise will help you do just that.

Place two chairs facing each other. Each partner must prepare a list beforehand of three things needed from your partner, three things wanted from your partner, three things you wish your partner would do for you, and three things your partner could do to make you laugh. These twelve things may be written seriously or with a light twist. For example:

Needs
1. I need you to tell me you love me more than life itself.
2. I need you to help me voluntarily as if I were your charitable contribution for the year.
3. I need you to approve of me more than you approve of winning the lottery.

Wants
1. I want you to spend more time with me.
2. I want to have sex with you several times a week without having to tie a blue ribbon around my genitals to prove my prowess.
3. I want to be able to talk with you without the staccato gunfire of interruption.

Wishes
1. I wish we could talk together with joy.
2. I wish you yearned for me to share my thoughts as Romeo yearned to know Juliet.
3. I wish you could see me as attractive no matter what sags, droops, bulges, or crinkles.

Laughs

1. You could help me laugh more by laughing with me when I laugh.
2. You could help me laugh more by watching comedies with me.
3. You could help me laugh more by playing with me the way you used to.

With your lists in hand, sit down facing each other. First, one partner reads his or her list and then the other. The listening partner may not comment during the reading of the partner's list. After reading the lists, clarify any questions with each other and discuss whatever comes up for you. Ask each other what you've learned about the other that you didn't know. At the end of the exercise give each other a playful, exuberant hug and say, "I hear you, I hear you, I hear you."

You have just communicated twelve very important things to each other. Talking one at a time without interruption insures both the talking and the listening for both of you. The laughter makes the experience fun and positive. Learning to listen carefully prevents many stupid misunderstandings. When we eliminate "Huh?" we also eliminate "Duh."

We laugh
because there is no other thing we can do about it.
Laughter erupts precisely
as the situation becomes hopeless.
—Walter Kerr

Chapter 5

IN THE BIG INNING,
There Were Sex, Money,
Children, and Housework

The laughter in our home is its heart beating.
Laughter leads us, kneads us
and sometimes helps bleed us of torments and woes.
—Bob Talbert

The Relationship team is in the playoffs. It's the final game between the issues that can bring a relationship to its knees and a couple's ability to laugh, have fun, and stay friends. The bases are loaded, and the issues are at bat. Money is on first, Children is on second, Housework is on third, and Sex is at the plate. The crowd is in an uproar of anticipation. The "Big Four" that lead the potential fighting lineup of every relationship are threatening victory again. A homerun with the bases loaded means that all four issues will once more add to the misery and possible demise of a relationship.

Sex, money, children, and housework are the heavy hitters couples fight over most of the time. One or all of these issues can stay at bat consistently if couples allow this to happen. Generally, there are deeper problems affecting relationships other than these four things, but partners' feelings seem to consistently play out in these particular arenas. Couples routinely focus their anger, dissatisfaction, disapproval and criticism on these four areas. Most men and women are not even aware that they are really fighting about deeper needs and wishes like control, approval, and appreciation. As their unresolved feelings about the deeper things allow the surface issues to become more powerful over time, the "runs" against a good relationship add up until the score is heavily against fun, laughter, and companionship. If couples allow the surface issues to hit too many homers, a good, potentially lasting relationship can lose the game.

It's important, however, that relationship fans don't lose heart. Laughter is a long time player in the game of "love me or leave me" and can certainly step up to the plate and save the day. Given a chance, laughter helps partners keep their balance in the relationship and helps them keep sex, money, children, and housework in perspective. After laughter has been at bat, if you listen carefully, you will hear the crowd cheering and laughing as the relationship walks away a winner. It is always important to remember to play the Big Four with Laughter as both coach and player in order to deal with things less seriously. And since Sex is currently at the plate in the relationship game going on in this chapter, let's pitch Laughter against the sexual issues in relationships and see how we can strike them out.

Whipped Cream, Silly String, and Sex

When I need to cry, I think about my sex life;
when I need to laugh, I think about my sex life.
—Glenda Jackson

It was dark in the bedroom so Sandra couldn't see the stony look on Howie's face. He lay rigid, feeling furious and confused by Sandra's reaction to his sexual overtures. He felt frustrated physically and embarrassed by her rejection. He knew she used to find him attractive, and he yearned for the good old days filled with desire and lots of satisfying sex.

Sandra lay on her side next to Howie overwhelmed with guilt. She knew she had hurt him, but he always wanted sex when she was overtired and feeling unloved. Howie was seldom romantic anymore and kissing seemed to be a forgotten art no matter how often she asked for it. Howie liked sex to be quick and to the point, and she just didn't like sex with him anymore. She didn't find it enjoyable. She wished with all her heart that she and Howie could regain the physical tenderness and love they had once shared. She wanted to want him but did not know how to get back her physical desire.

Couples like Howie and Sandra are not unusual, and they usually don't know what to do about their unhappy sex lives. Sex is a huge issue in lots of relationships. Relationships that began with romantic sex often become relationships without romance and only perfunctory sex that really satisfies neither partner. As a result, sex becomes a serious issue, and it is no longer much fun. When sex is no longer fun or enjoyable, people don't easily seek it out. They need something pleasurable to pique their interest and stir their desire.

Laughter can be just the aphrodisiac people need to perk up their interest in sex and renew their sense that sex is fun. According to Dr. Debora Phillips, if people maintain a humorous perspective about sex, they will also maintain "a sense that the miraculous and the ridiculous are very closely related." If couples know this, it makes it okay to laugh during sex when something surprising, awkward, silly, or unpredictable happens. Laughter is an invaluable tool to help partners enjoy those uneasy sexual moments that they often encounter. When our bodies don't cooperate, we say the wrong thing, or we fumble at a crucial moment, laughter allows such personal, embarrassing idiosyncrasies to become special, intimate elements of love.

If people can laugh at themselves while performing the ever-serious rite of lovemaking, they are freer to be sexually more adventurous, more tolerant, and more fun. Because laughter is a marvelous form of intimacy in itself, it also helps couples effortlessly create the element of romance essential to good sex as well. By easing awkward moments, developing a sense of fun and adventure, and creating romance, laughter can balance any concerns about the more serious aspects of sex like physical release, performance, and procreation.

Serious Sex is usually driven by biological need. Since men normally have a stronger sex drive than women, they tend to initiate Serious Sex more often. It is unfortunate for both sexes that men seldom see their sexual needs as a laughing matter. Therefore, as sex gradually becomes more serious in a relationship and becomes an expectation rather than an art, many men not only forego laughter but also bypass other preliminaries of the mating ritual. As a result, sex loses some of its softness and intimacy.

Although men need love as much as women, they generally have less need for intimacy and romance. Therefore, they are apt to let the romantic aspects of sex slide by the wayside. Many men see no need to continue to woo their partner once they are in a committed relationship. They have succeeded in finding a mate who, to their way of thinking, was the sole purpose of romance and pursuit. Once a mate is secured, men tend to expect their partners to become sexually more like themselves and go right to the heart of the matter with little preliminary warm-up. Most women, however, want that warm-up because it makes them feel loved. Many men dissociate sex and love, perceiving sex as only sex and not a way of showing their wives that they love them. It's as if the security of commitment causes a memory glitch for men, and they fail to remember that women are different from them in what they appreciate about sex.

Unlike men, women tend to hate instant sex. Most females need romance as their biological trigger for sex, and they require romance to peak their interest sexually both before and after commitment. Contrary to some men's expectations, female sexual triggers don't change because they find a permanent partner. The following contemporary joke underscores the importance of ongoing romance and the danger of taking a woman's sex drive for granted.

Question: What food do women eat that affects the level of their sex drive?

Answer: Wedding cake.

Just as the male peacock spreads its tail feathers to attract the female every time it wants to mate, men need to continue providing romance to attract their female partners time after time.

It is interesting to note that some men who really love their wives still resist the idea of ongoing romance even when the need for it is brought to their attention. For example, when encouraged to provide more romance for his wife, Al justified his reluctance by saying that when he was young, kissing was all of sex to him. Once he experienced the real thing, he saw no need to kiss or engage in other forms of romance. It seemed a waste of time. From the time of his first experience with "real sex," he has wanted to "get right to it," and he can't understand why his wife Cindy doesn't want to also. Cindy explained to him that romance makes her feel loved, and love enhances her sexual desire. She doesn't want to "get right to it" and resents the fact that Al wants that from her. Because of this struggle between the two, sex is a barrier to happiness for Al and Cindy. Unfortunately, they are not alone. Other couples find sex a complex, unending struggle as well.

Like Al and Cindy, Jim and Allison are another example of a young couple with very big issues between them. Sex was simply on the top of the heap. They were very serious about sex most of the time because they had completely opposite feelings about it. Jim wanted sex all the time and pushed his beautiful, young wife to give it to him. She disliked sex most of the time and resisted saying yes to his sexual invitations. They were an actual manifestation of the different gender perceptions of sex. Man: We almost never have sex—only two or three times a week. Woman: We have sex constantly—two or three times a week. As a result of their differences, Jim and Allison argued about sex a lot.

During a therapy session where they were seeking solutions to their problems, Jim was amazed to hear that women need romance to become aroused. Allison told him she needed and wanted romance every single time. Looking as if she had told him he had to drink castor oil instead of providing her with romance, Jim defended his lack of romance by saying that in the movies women want sex just as much as men and just as quickly. The women portrayed in movies don't care about romance, so he did not think Allison should either.

Both Jim and Allison had movie images of what sex should be like. Allison expected Jim to epitomize romance and constantly make her feel loved and desirable like the heroine of a romantic movie. Jim expected Allison to desire sex twenty-four hours a day and with such intensity that she could barely resist throwing herself atop him at the grocery store.

Their unrealistic expectations of each other and their resistance to those expectations kept them frustrated and apart. Laughter in their sex life could have bridged the distance between them and opened up lots of different options that were more practical than the single option on which they each focused. Unfortunately, laughter was not often a part of their sex life. There were rare occasions, however, when they actually made quality time for each other and approached sex positively. During those times, they instinctively incorporated creative games into sex, and they reported that the games created much laughter and fun between them. Unfortunately for Jim and Allison, such fun was the exception rather than the rule. Because of their power struggle, sex was usually a serious battleground instead of a lighthearted playground.

Although Serious Sex is not necessarily a battle between partners, it is often somewhat like work. Viewing sex as work, an obligation, or just a bodily function causes it to hold little ongoing appeal for most people. A quick sexual encounter, crammed in only when your other responsibilities allow it, makes sex little more fun than gulping down a meal, taking a quick bath, ironing your clothes, or using the bathroom.

If, however, couples create a sex life that incorporates fun, laughter, and romance, they elevate sex to an activity both partners really want to do and look forward to doing. When it comes to combining sex and fun, however, couples are on their own. Our culture doesn't offer much help in approaching sex as fun. While there is a relentless focus on sex in advertising, movies, and television, it is seldom portrayed as fun. Sex is generally depicted as serious passion that, if we're lucky, may elicit smiles after both partners are satisfied. As obsessed as we are by sex culturally, we're also so serious about it that we actually believe we can't laugh about our own sex lives. We think we must distance sex from ourselves personally, so we only allow ourselves to laugh at other people's sexual foibles.

Even as we "peep" at sex that is not our own in movies, television, and literature, we don't allow ourselves to see the remains of everyday sexual relationships that litter our immediate landscape. We are quite unaware of the fact that while seated before our television sets, we consciously and unconsciously receive a steady diet of sexual ideas that perpetuate a deadly common myth. We learn and believe with fervent rigidity that sex must be spontaneous to be good. We virtually worship at the altar of sexual spontaneity even though it is to our own detriment. Because of different time schedules, responsibilities, and physical energy, mutual spontaneity is hard to achieve. However, so rigidly do we hold to this particular value people choose to have no sex rather than planned sex. Choosing to have no sex puts nails in the coffin of many relationships that are healthy otherwise.

In order to solve this problem, we need to look the myth of sexual spontaneity in the face and make it fun instead of making it sacred. With a little flexibility of thought and action, partners can easily solve the problem of no sex due to a lack of spontaneity. They can set up sexual appointments. An appointment to have sex with the one you love is a shocking idea to many but actually serves to take the pressure off both partners in a relationship. If couples choose specific times for sex that work for both of them, put it on their schedules, and follow through, sexual frustrations will slip away. Partners will no longer have to deal with the annoyance of being unwillingly awakened in the night or at the crack of dawn or being turned down due to fatigue.

With sex appointments, one gets to anticipate, plan, and enjoy a sexual encounter with one's partner just as one did when the relationship was new. A sex appointment is really much the same as planning sex when dating and takes away none of the enjoyment. When arranging sexual dates with your partner, however, it is important to keep this bit of "tongue in cheek" wisdom in mind. Be sure you make the dates yourself. Don't slip up and have your secretary call to make the appointment for you....

Even after you and your partner choose to set up sexual appointments, all sexual spontaneity is not taboo. Couples continue to need and use spontaneous sex signals to indicate ongoing sexual interest. Men and women need to know their partners find them attractive even if they are having regular sex appointments. Sex signals must not be allowed to fall by the wayside as relationships mature. You can prevent this problem by devising and maintaining effective sex signals for your partner with just a bit of flexibility and creativity. This is the same flexibility and creativity that enable people to be playful in the pursuit of sex. Therefore, sex signals are an area of sex made for fun. Enjoyable, effective sex signals can be verbal, nonverbal, or a combination of both. The more creative and less serious they are the better.

The actress, Mae West, was famous for her verbal approaches to sex like, " Hey, big boy, is that a gun in your pocket or are you glad to see me?" If you like verbal signals, you can follow her lead with a similar, naughty kind of verbal wit. If nonverbal signals are preferred, you might choose to do things like winking at each other, rubbing each other's foot, raising your eyebrows comically and suggestively, or peeping seductively over the newspaper. You are only limited in your choice of sex signals by your own imagination and sense of play. For example, a particularly creative woman named Hannah put the little red flag from a mailbox on her bathroom mirror. When the flag was up, she was in the mood. When it was down, she was not in the mood. It was an imaginative sex signal that worked well for her and her husband.

Phillip and Marge were a couple who developed a playful sex signal they both enjoyed and used for years. It not only signaled sex but also enabled them to begin their sexual encounters with a smile. Phillip would say, "I see two grapefruit." Marge would respond with, "I see a banana." Then, together they would chorus, "Do you want to play fruit basket turn over?" Another imaginative couple with a sense of humor signaled sex by asking each other if it was time to "play the organ." That usually got a grin from the one being asked, and the fun could begin.

In addition to sex appointments and creative sex signals, couples can put fun into their sex life by playing sexual games with one another. The games can be simple and uncomplicated or more complex if preferred. The only requirement is that they be fun. They do not have to be abnormal or extremely unusual. For example, one couple created a game called "You Move, You Lose." In the game, one person kisses the other all over in an effort to make them wiggle. The recipient of the kisses must try to lie totally still. If unable to lie still, he or she loses and has to provide the winner with one of his or her heart's desires. According to the couple playing "You Move, You Lose," they laughed a great deal and enjoyed themselves immensely. It was fun for both winner and loser.

Creating sexual games can be both exciting and fun. Although you will want to develop your own special ways of playing sexually, another example of a game couples can play is taking turns telling each other what you want sexually and enjoying each other providing it. Playing strip poker also has possibilities for sexual fun, and wearing clown noses during sex can certainly lighten things up. Some people find it even funnier to think of wearing clown noses on other parts of the body in addition to the nose.

Sex and fun are a great combination that can put Serious Sex out at home plate. If couples put enjoyment into their sex life, it not only becomes more exciting to do but much easier to talk about. Ironically, in our society we are embarrassed to talk openly about sex even though we use it in advertising to sell everything from chewing gum to toilet paper. Our sexual embarrassment is a very real issue that makes it hard to talk with our partners about sex. Since laughter relieves embarrassment, the more laughter we incorporate into our sex lives, the

Marriage is an institution.
Marriage is love. Love is blind.
Therefore marriage is an institution
for the blind.

— Sewanee Mountain Goat

less anxious we feel. Therefore, what were once embarrassing barriers between partners can become shared secrets, and as a result, they can talk things out when they need to. Also, as laughter relieves our embarrassment during sex, it gives partners easier passage through all those awkward sexual moments that can occur. It draws couples closer together and provides the platform for a good, lasting sex life.

In for a Penny, In for a Pound

> There is no jovial companionship equal to that where the jokes are rather small and the laughter abundant.
> —Washington Irving

In addition to sexual issues, couples frequently have serious difficulty over money. There are many reasons for this: different monetary values, emotional needs connected to money, childhood issues about money, gender issues about money, and control issues. In the beginning of a relationship, money is seldom a problem. Any concerns about it are overshadowed by the thrill of being in love and by the "blindness" that goes along with it. Therefore, after a couple settles into their relationship, they are often surprised that money becomes the golden peg on which they hang their arguing hat. Powerful differences can exist that make it difficult to manage the financial aspects of a relationship amicably.

Although there are exceptions to every generalization, money has culturally come to mean power to men and security to women. Although both sexes enjoy some sense of power and security where money is concerned, the stronger emphasis on one or the other determines both feelings and behavior regarding money. For example, in giving men a sense of power and freedom, money helps them meet their need to compete with other people. It allows them to maintain the impression that money is no big deal. The desire to appear financially independent is so strong that men will often buy rounds of drinks and pick up dinner tabs whether they can afford them or not. They need to present the image of financial freedom, particularly to other men. The need is so powerful that it creates spending patterns in men that can place a strain on their relationships.

Money certainly placed a strain on Bart and Sally's relationship. When Bart's niece and her family were in town, Bart and Sally went to dinner with them and another couple. While at dinner, Bart allowed himself to be trapped in a typical male quandary. Although plans were carefully made ahead of time to go "dutch" for dinner, when it came time to pay the sizeable tab, one of the other guys undermined Bart's intention by volunteering to treat everyone to dinner by splitting the tab with Bart. Unfortunately, the man had not consulted with Bart before making the offer.

Bart, who did not have the money to pay half the tab, still felt obligated to go along with the other man or be mortally embarrassed. Sally, on the other hand, could not understand why he didn't take the other man aside and tell him he did not want to share the tab. An argument between Bart and Sally ensued later over what Bart should have done about the dinner bill. Although they argued about the money, the real argument was over Bart's fear of embarrassment and Sally's anxiety about how they would pay for the subsequent bill. Since they were unaware of the real issues for each of them, the argument was futile in resolving the problem and left both of them feeling tense and angry.

Obviously, an unexpected bill of several hundred dollars was not a laughing matter for Bart and Sally. Also, at this point in their lives, they were not using much humor as a means of coping with serious problems. Since they were engaged in a power struggle over money, it was an ongoing source of conflict for them, and they could not find a way to discuss the situation effectively from a serious point of view. If they had been able to see just a tiny bit of a lighter side to the problem like facetiously blaming their credit cards for allowing people on a "peasant income" to act like they are wealthy, they would probably have been better able to discuss the incident with at least some understanding of their individual concerns. They could have talked together on a practical level, one peasant to another.

Needless to say, this particular incident for Bart and Sally was only the tip of their monetary iceberg. Both of them were emotional spenders who soothed depression by buying wanted, but unnecessary, things that added to their financial debt. Each criticized the other for his or her behavior, and they drew battle lines every month when it came time to pay the bills. Their underlying, unmet needs for appreciation, approval and support kept them from working together. Instead, they battled for control by refusing to help each other. Instead of feelings of love for one another, they developed a strong sense of mistrust and a great deal of anxiety.

Bart and Sally finally decided to seek counseling as a solution to their marital issues. To their delight, they were encouraged to work on their problems with laughter, and they began to develop ways to lighten up about money. At first, their minds went totally blank on how to do this because laughter and money did not seem to go together. They had real trouble deciding how they could become more playful about what had always been a serious issue. As they sat in silence and looked at each other, they each seemed so miserably puzzled that they spontaneously burst out laughing. Bart commented that since they were paying money for help, you would think they would have many ideas. With a twinkle in his eye, he said,

"Maybe we should fight over who pays for the session to get our creative juices going." They laughed again, and the ideas on how to lighten up about money finally began to flow, uncorked by their laughter.

Bart and Sally first began to reduce the seriousness of money in their relationship by hanging a picture of a dollar bill with a mustache, a beard, and a smile drawn on George Washington's face on their back door. Under it, they wrote, "After all, it is only money." Secondly, they decided to try to ease the stress of paying their bills by turning it into a romantic evening. They cooked a nice dinner, lit the candles, and put on romantic music. After dinner, they paid their bills together. After writing a few checks, they engaged in a passionate kiss and said together, "Yum-m-m-my. Kissing, money, and love." The silliness of it made them laugh. They continued their fun until the bills were all paid. The romance involved allowed them to finish paying the bills and then go off to bed with something other than bills on their minds.

In addition to connecting bill paying and romance, Bart and Sally also made up a list of ideas on how to stay light about the issue of money. That way, when one idea lost its charm, they had another idea to take its place. They found that the more they played with money, the more creative they became. As their laughter and good feelings took hold, they were able to discuss the realistic aspects of money management without fighting. They seriously compared their value systems and identified the areas of agreement and disagreement. They found, for example, that they agreed with each other that they should pay the bills before they spent money on pleasure. They disagreed on what things were worth large expenditures. Sally felt it was okay to spend lots of money on clothes. Bart preferred to spend money on electronic devices and his motorcycle. As they identified the areas of agreement and disagreement, they also developed ways to compromise and created a system of dealing with money that was more supportive and satisfying. Money became an issue much less often.

If couples like Bart and Sally could identify and understand what money means to them, they would be one step closer to resolving the issue. Our feelings and values about money are ingrained when we are young. Growing up without enough money, for example, can either cause a person to save money compulsively or conversely, spend money compulsively. Such behavior develops in response to our upbringing. The over-spender may have felt deprived growing up and makes up for it by spending. The compulsive saver, on the other hand, also felt deprived growing up but now fears being without money and is compelled to save for rainy days.

In addition to such environmental circumstances, our parents' emphasis on how to handle money also strongly impacts us. We learn to handle money from them. Their values are imposed on us, and we often make them our own. As a result of environment and parenting, we all develop strong values and opinions about money. Some of our opinions are conscious, and some are unconscious. It's the unconscious opinions that generally keep the money issue dangerously stirred up between couples because they come into play disguised as something else, as they did for Bart and Sally.

In addition to all the messages about money that we get from our families, society adds to the financial stress for couples by teaching men to handle money one way and women another. For instance, men traditionally use money to take care of people, particularly their wives and families. They also tend to use money to keep up with the Joneses. Women, on the other hand, use money to feel secure and are traditionally more cautious about spending to keep up with the Joneses. They would rather feel safe than equal. Women are also scrupulously fair about money when out with other people. They divide the check down to the penny. Men are much less "picky" about money and may just split the tab equally or take turns picking up the tab. As a result of such differences, working out compromises between saving and spending is tricky for most couples and requires the development of a system that works for both partners.

Because of the overt and covert messages about money that we receive and because of the power it has to give us what we want and need, money is an emotional issue for all of us. By using the following test, you can begin to identify your emotional issues about money.

1. Check the items that apply to you and put a **P** or an **S** beside them to represent power or security. This will identify which major money issue is most important to you.
2. After each item checked, ask yourself this question: "Why does this represent power or security to me?"
3. Write your answers down. This will help you identify your individual values about money.
4. If your partner will participate with you, you can also compare values.

Money Test

1. _____ I feel in control when I have money in my pocket or purse.

2. _____ I feel safe when I know I have enough money.

3. _____ I like the way I feel when I can buy whatever I want.

4. _____ It's important to have money for my needs and my family's needs.

5. _____ I must have the ability to afford a nice vacation for my family.

6. _____ I like buying large items more than small ones.

7. _____ I like the illusion of never-ending money that I

get from credit cards.

8. _____ I spend money whether I can afford it or not.

9. _____ It's important to me to have money to buy gifts for others.

10. _____ It's important to me to pay my bills.

11. _____ It's important to me to have money to buy meals and/or drinks for others.

12. _____ I spend money freely even when I'm in debt.

13. _____ I hate to be criticized about my spending habits.

14. _____ The need for money makes me anxious.

15. _____ The lack of money embarrasses me.

16. _____ I need to have money to spend freely without consulting anyone.

17. _____ I need to be able to trust my partner about money.

18. _____ I am generous with money.

19. _____ I am stingy with money.

20. _____ My fondest dream is winning the lottery.

After taking this test, you should have some important, serious information about the role of money in your relationship. Having information about money can serve as a basis for you to begin to find ways to laugh about it. You can begin the process of lightening up by bouncing your ideas, funny or not, off each other. You might say something ridiculous to your partner like, "In order to make extra money, let's consider disguising ourselves as money baskets and then stand by the toll booths at the airport and catch quarters." Another facetious idea to acquire money is to suggest that you ask for the pennies left beside cash registers. You can imagine simply telling the cashier, "We're broke" as you scoop up the coins. Let your creativity run. Make a list of your ideas no matter how outrageous or silly. Sift through them together and begin to implement one or two that seem to add fun to the issue of money for both of you.

After listing laughter ideas, mix in ideas about expressing love with money. One of you might say, "A penny for your thoughts" and the other will reply, "I was thinking about how much I love you." Tell each other how you would use inherited money to show your love— a love boat cruise, for example. With enough of these mixed ideas of silliness and love, you should begin to associate money with laughter, fun, and love. What could be a great big issue of greed and control can become a means of support, approval, and enjoyment. A "Scroogified" attitude will give way to an attitude of "God bless us one and all." In the American South, a Yankee Dime is a kiss. You can clue your partner into your need for a kiss by telling him or her that you need to visit the "dime" store. If you can start collecting Yankee Dimes from each other, and take them to the emotional bank, you'll both be a lot richer.

Hanging from the Family Tree

A good laugh is sunshine in a house.
—William Thackeray

In addition to sex and money, the third major issue couples fight over is children. It's easy for parents to lock down in disagreement over methods of discipline or who is responsible for various aspects of child care. Once again, it is important to remember that the power struggle over our children is rooted in our own histories. For example, if we had strict parents, we may feel it's essential to be strict ourselves. We frequently tend to do to our children what was done to us whether we want to or not. In a crisis, that is often the only thing that pops into our minds, and we act upon it. However, if something our parents did really hurt us, we may dwell on it enough that we do the opposite of what they did to us. If we were abused as children, for example, we may be exceptionally lenient with our own children. All parents bring emotional baggage and strong opinions into the area of child care, and if they are not in agreement about their basic rules of child rearing, these opinions can result in a great deal of conflict between the parents and confusion for the children.

Ernest and Barbara, for instance, often found themselves at odds over their children. Barbara took an active role with the children and spent a great deal of time with them. However, she was not consistent in her discipline and sometimes had trouble controlling the children. Ernest, on the other hand, was more distant from the kids than his wife and didn't spend a lot of time interacting with them in a positive manner. He was a strict disciplinarian, however, and criticized Barbara regularly for not being stronger and more consistent.

Because of their different ways of dealing with their children, Ernest and Barbara argued frequently about who was right and who was wrong. They often undermined each other with the children and blamed each other for the children's misbehavior. Each felt the other saw him as an inadequate or bad parent. It was one more area in their relationship where each felt criticized and incapable. The arguments over the children pushed them farther apart and played a role in the children's ability to manipulate them.

Because of her own childhood, Barbara craved a close family without criticism and bitterness. In her desperation to meet her need, she pushed Ernest to be more involved, and he responded by drifting further away. Interestingly, Ernest had had a childhood similar to the one he was providing for his children. Although he did not like his own childhood because he had often felt unloved, he seemed unable to stop treating his children the way he was treated. In fact, like his father, he disliked and distanced himself the most from the child who was the most like him. Ernest's behavior is not uncommon in parents. We often reject in our children those aspects of ourselves we find least acceptable.

Ironically, Barbara found the same child Ernest disliked to be the hardest for her to like because the child was so much like Ernest and like Barbara's own mother. Because of her internal struggle to like this child whom she knew she loved, Barbara tried to please her daughter by meeting the child's demands in order to keep the peace. Ernest coped by trying to manhandle the child, and "the peace be damned." Needless to say, Ernest and Barbara found little enjoyment in raising their children.

After finally being pushed to the wall by all their unresolved issues, Barbara and Ernest sought help. Of all the options available to them, they found the idea of healing with laughter to be the most appealing and hopeful. They signed up for a laughter seminar and began the process of trying to regain their love, approval, and intimacy through increasing the laughter and fun in their relationship.

Barbara and Ernest worked on all their issues beginning with the raising of their children. As they focused on changing the way they worked with their children, they began by writing down all the good things they both had to offer as parents. They looked at how their individual strengths could support the other's weaknesses, and then, they formulated a plan to interact positively with the children as a team. For example, Ernest would handle some of the discipline but only after consulting Barbara, who would temper his tendency to be too harsh. Barbara would organize family events in such a way that it would be easy for Ernest to participate. As they began to parent as a team, a magical transformation took place. The children's behavior became more manageable, and Ernest and Barbara felt less anxious about most of their parental decisions. It wasn't all a bed of roses, of course, but they felt a lot better about themselves and their children.

In addition to employing teamwork in parenting, Barbara and Ernest began to actively work at remembering the humorous incidents that had taken place with their children. As they remembered different incidents and laughed together, they felt enjoyment at being in the parenting game together. One incident they remembered and laughed about was finding their two small children covered in flour in the middle of the kitchen floor where they had been making snow angels. Retelling many of the cute and funny things their children had done reminded them that parenting could be fun as well as frustrating.

As their feelings about parenting improved, Ernest and Barbara agreed to play together with their children for at least one hour per week. They also talked about creating a home video of their children's funniest moments. With their creativity flowing and parenting no longer a point of conflict, Barbara and Ernest had begun the happy journey of raising their children together with fun and laughter. Without the constant tension of each other's criticism, they were also able to discuss the serious aspects of discipline and daily child care with greater openness. Their problem solving became easier and more effective when the children were no longer the focus in a power struggle.

Although children are not always the focal point in a power struggle as they were for Ernest and Barbara, the normal arguing parents do over child care has been raised to new heights by divorce and remarriage. Raising one's own children is a challenge, but raising someone else's children can be a monumental challenge. Many factors make it hard on both the parents and the children. In divorce and remarriage, children experience divided loyalties, anxiety about permanence, and the hassle of traveling back and forth between parents. They often don't know how to feel about their parents' divorce or a new stepparent they did not choose but are expected to love.

On their part, parents expect things of themselves and their partners that aren't realistic in a blended family. Women often expect stepfathers to immediately take over the discipline as soon as the marriage takes place. Children resent it, and that makes it harder for the stepfather to form a good relationship with his stepchildren. Men, on the other hand, frequently expect stepmothers to move easily into the nurturing role for the stepchildren, and once again, children often resent it. Children and stepparents require time to build relationships with each other, and until that takes place, the biological parent should see to the needs of his or her own children.

While stepparents and stepchildren struggle with forming a relationship, the parents themselves often lock into a power struggle based on childhood issues, cultural biases, and an accentuated feeling of self righteousness because *I am the real parent*. Trying to form a successful blended family can become a very serious business. The seriousness then makes it even harder for family members to like each other, interact positively and form a new, successful family unit.

If the couple forming the blended family maintains laughter and fun during the parenting process, the new family will form more easily and develop a more positive identity of its own. Unlike one child's description of marriage, holy matrimony doesn't have to become holy acrimony. New families can be formed where family members love each other and adjust positively to the changes brought by divorce and remarriage.

Unfortunately, a positive adjustment had not been the case for Tina and Joe after they married. They were a couple who endured a very serious attempt to have a blended family. Problems had occurred between parents and children and between biological children and stepchildren. The situation had grown worse and worse until the family was emotionally divided, and there were few positive feelings among the family members. The entire blended family included Tina's two teenage daughters, Joe's preteen son, Tina and Joe's two-year-old son, and Tina and Joe.

As things grew worse, the family finally polarized into three factions including Tina and her teenaged daughters, Joe and his preteen son, and Joe, Tina, and the toddler. Not only was the situation tense, it was confusing to everyone, and anger was the emotion of the day. When Tina and Joe were finally exasperated to the point of considering divorce, they realized it was time to search for other options. They had friends who had found help for their relationship by attending a laughter workshop for couples. Tina and Joe decided to try Laughter Therapy for their own relationship since they were desperate for relief, and laughter certainly sounded appealing.

One of the first things Joe and Tina learned to do that would reintegrate laughter into their lives was to practice laughing. They began faking laughter for no reason at all. It felt awkward and silly at first, but they persevered anyway. After a while, it began to be fun. They laughed in the car, the grocery store, the shopping mall, and in the bedroom. As they continued laughing, fake laughter often gave way to real laughter. They found it became easier to laugh at will. They were on their way to becoming Liberated Laughers—people who have the ability to laugh easily and often.

Their children criticized the laughter at first but then began to feel their own need to laugh. It became too hard for them to stay consistently critical, angry, and serious. They began to laugh more with their parents as well as with one another. In addition to laughing more, Joe, Tina, and the children also began looking at movies and television shows that made them laugh. Joe and Tina learned to enjoy reading books to each other that were light in content. They also began to look for and enjoy the everyday humor they found at home as well as away from home. The laughter created by Joe and Tina began to change the general atmosphere in the home, and the tension level dropped.

To encourage even more laughter and to further ease the tension around serious issues, Joe and Tina also purchased clown noses for all family members. When tense subjects were being discussed, they agreed as a family that the person talking would wear the nose. This took the sting out of any negative words and allowed the rest of the family to hear the person talking with little or no defensiveness. Despite fears to the contrary, the noses did not diminish the importance of what was being discussed. They just helped keep anger under control. The family didn't always laugh, but the noses cut way down on the yelling. It's difficult to be angry with someone wearing a clown nose.

In addition to using the clown noses to talk seriously, the family also found tons of fun ways to use their clown noses at home and in public. They stuck them on when checking out in stores and acted as if nothing were out of the ordinary. People in line couldn't help themselves.

They started smiling and asking questions. Strangers became friends, and the fun was shared with others. Of course, the teenagers also wore some extra noses as earrings just to be a little different and more noticeable. The clown noses themselves prompted creativity and fun for the family that seemed to grow unabated.

Along with the laughter and clown noses, Tina and Joe worked to put play into their parenting. They turned decision making into a contest. They kept score of whose decisions turned out to be good ones, and the one to reach fifty points first got the parenting prize of a night out. They slowly began to change their interaction with each other's children. Their parenting became something positive and a bit lighter in approach and attitude.

Tina and Joe's children slowly began to respond to the positive changes their parents were making. The lighter atmosphere made an impact on them despite their adolescent skepticism. There were no miracles in the house, and bonds among them were not forged overnight. However, they did begin to like each other better, and the foundation of a more positive blended family slowly emerged amidst giggles, laughs, and positive interaction with each other. The bonding of laughter and its power to heal worked magic in Joe and Tina's relationship and in their family as well.

No one is saying that laughter takes the place of good parenting, but it is a part of good parenting. If parents look at child care as a team project that's fun, it is far less likely to become an issue in the relationship. Children can certainly be stressors in their parents' lives. If, however, couples remember to see the humor in the situations that occur with their children and sprinkle the family liberally with laughter, children do not have to be a big issue between the parents. Parenting can be fun and a great source of joy and happiness.

A Maid! A Maid!
Our Kingdom for a Maid!

There are three ways to get something done;
do it yourself, hire someone, or forbid your kids to do it.
—Monta Crane

In this modern age of two working partners, a fourth issue has begun besieging couples along with sex, money, and children. The newest issue couples fight over consistently is housework. In times past, our respective genders came with clearly defined roles and responsibilities in relationships. That is no longer true. Women are now working to contribute money to the relationship, and they need men to help with the housework.

Changes are never easy in societies, but this change seems more painful than many others. Women have trouble asking men for help around the house and often agonize in guilt when they do. Generally, men still expect to go to work, do the outside work, take care of the car and leave the housework for the women. As a result, women feel overwhelmed, unappreciated, and unloved. They no longer feel taken care of by the men, and they no longer feel things are fair. The resulting friction is taking its toll on relationships.

As women maneuver indirectly for help in true feminine fashion, men feel manipulated and angry. They aren't clear about what their partners want or need, and as long as they exist in a fuzzy lack of clarity, many men tend to do little or nothing around the house. Few people enjoy housework enough to do it cheerfully, and as anger and irritation for men and women grow ever more serious around this issue, relationships are in danger.

Lucy was one of those overwhelmed, unappreciated,

and, finally, angry women. After years in a household with all men, she could take it no longer. She walked out. Her pleas for help had fallen on the deaf ears of her spouse for twenty years. She had tried to keep order in the home with a husband and two male children who didn't care and didn't help. Tired from her job, her housework, and finally her marriage, she sought refuge alone.

Mark was thunderstruck. He could not believe that she would leave him over housework. He had no understanding of her feelings and could not see where he had failed her. As the housework fell on his shoulders after her departure, the light slowly began to dawn. He asked her to go with him for counseling to save their relationship, and she agreed. In the midst of all her turmoil and rage, she knew she still loved him and wanted to stay with him if possible.

In the course of their counseling, Laughter Therapy was introduced to them, and they decided to try it. Mark and Lucy were amazed to realize how serious they had become about housework as well as other things. Their serious approach to their relationship in general had squelched the fun in their lives and buried much of their love beneath anger and apathy.

Lucy agreed to return home, and she and Mark specifically began to look for ways to have fun with the housework issue so they could laugh about it more. They decided to develop a housework triathlon competition. They each took on two major weekly household chores and one daily chore. The first one to finish the daily chore on all seven days got a day off. The first one to finish the weekly chores got to have the dinner of his or her choice with no cooking, delivery, or cleanup responsibilities at all. If one of them won the entire triathlon, he or she got fifty dollars to use frivolously.

In addition to turning housework into a friendly competition, Mark and Lucy put more fun into it by dressing up the vacuum cleaner as a maid. They made her a nice lace apron and cap to wear when she sucked dust. They occasionally put bubble bath in the dishwater for extra bubbles and for a fun smell. They also added fun by cleaning the bathrooms together in the "buff" and celebrated the conclusion of that chore by taking a shower together in their sparkling, clean shower. They found they could learn to love cleaning bathrooms. They also hung bubble-blowing liquid around their necks when cleaning and every now and then paused to blow bubbles.

As the housework became challenging fun, they ironically learned to look forward to it. They worked as a team and felt their feelings toward one another shift. Mark and Lucy both felt more appreciated and loved. While helping each other do the housework, they complimented each other lavishly on what a good job they were doing. Housework shrank as an issue between them as their other needs for love and appreciation were met, and they supported each other as a couple. As a final touch to remind them to keep things light when it came to cooking and cleaning, they stuck the following poem on their refrigerator door.

> Mary had a little lamb.
> Now the lamb is dead.
> But we can use it anyhow
> To see that we are fed.

Such a light touch can remind us all that housework is just one more responsibility couples need to share. It's important to get it done, but it should not take precedence over taking care of the relationship. As long as couples nourish their relationships with laughter, love, and fun, issues like sex, money, children, and housework will not create the kind of power struggles that can ruin the relationship. Facing responsibilities together with a light-hearted focus will keep relationships healthy and full of love, and everyone is a winner.

In conclusion, as we return our attention to our ball game between laughter and the four big issues of relationships, we find the game is over. The shadows have lengthened on the baseball field, and cleaning crews are moving through the empty stands picking up after the fans of good relationships. The score is still on the scoreboard. Relationships – four, The Big Four – zero. Once again, laughter has saved the day. It has livened up sex lives, diminished greed, drawn families closer together, and turned housework into fun. Although the roar of the crowd's enthusiasm for laughter is now only a memory, echoes of the voices of the cheerleaders seem to linger still. "Laughter, Laughter, he's our man. If he can't do it, no one can." Meanwhile, outside in their cars, laughing couples are driving home from the game with more love in their hearts.

Exercise

Pla-a-ay Ball!!

Developing fun, effective ways of dealing with serious issues is not always easy. We create rigid ways of looking at our issues, and laughter and fun don't always come readily to mind. The following exercise can be useful in getting your creative juices flowing in order to lighten up on "The Big Four."

1. Get a ball of some kind, preferably one that does not engender competition. Beach balls and nerf balls are always good choices. Throwing a ball creates instant play and laughter and diverts adults from feeling too silly.
2. Stand apart facing one another.
3. For the warm up, the partner with the ball throws it to the other and calls out one of the issues like Housework.
4. The partner catching the ball must think of something good about the issue and call it out. Then he or she throws the ball back calling out an issue, and the partner must say a good thing.
5. After saying a few good things has set your minds in a positive direction and catching and throwing the ball have created a playful attitude, change the rules so the partner catching the ball must now come up with a fun way to work on the issue together.
6. Do this for all four major issues.
7. After developing a few ideas, stop and write them down for the future. Develop a running list of ideas to use when needed. Continue playing as long as it is fun.
8. After using the exercise, take a moment to notice how you feel about the four big issues now. Share those feelings with one another. Has your per-

spective changed? Can you discuss the issues more calmly and clearly? Do you feel good about each other?

Shared laughter creates a bond of friendship.
—W. Lee Grant

Laughter relieves emotional constipation.

Chapter 6

You Can't Rain on My Parade

There are three things which are real:
God, human folly and laughter.
The first two are beyond our comprehension,
so we must do what we can with the third.
—John F. Kennedy

Andrea felt her face aching again, and realized she was clenching her jaws as she thought about her husband. They had been married for five years, and the relationship no longer brought her joy. She loved Ted and believed he loved her, but it just wasn't fun to be around him anymore. Over the years, he had become increasingly solemn. He seldom laughed or cracked a joke, and he refused to do anything fun. It took an act of God just to get him to pay attention to her in a way that made her feel remotely accepted and loved. Consequently, she frequently found herself in the emotional dilemma of deciding whether she could continue to live this way. Loving him sometimes seemed less important than finding joy in living.

Andrea had grown up in a household full of laughter. Her family had its share of problems like every other family, but the problems were nicely balanced by the laughter. When she first met Ted, he loved her sense of humor and her easy laugh. He was drawn to her ability to laugh about important things because he tended to be so serious. Andrea found his dry sense of humor attractive and frankly, as she thought about it now, she was also attracted to his love of her own laughter and attitude toward life. It's hard to resist that kind of adoration.

After they married, however, their senses of humor no longer seemed to maintain the attraction between them, and she somehow misplaced her old devil-may-care attitude. She also misplaced her easy laughter. As Andrea mused about her relationship, she found herself thinking that she wanted her laughter back. I refuse to live life as a sourpuss, she thought. It's no fun, and the stress makes my face hurt. If I am going to stay with Ted, I have to find a way to laugh more in spite of him. She felt it was crucial to begin laughing again, or she wasn't sure she could tolerate the marriage. Lately, being in the relationship had felt like attending a daily funeral, and she was afraid if she didn't act soon, it would feel like a funeral where she was the corpse.

Living with a Serious Partner

Life is not a laughing matter...
but can you imagine having to live without laughing?
—Leonid Sukhorukov

Like Andrea, many of us find ourselves unwittingly married to someone who is serious about everything and has no desire to change. If we want a livelier lifestyle with more fun and laughter, what do we do then? Assuming we love our partner and don't want a divorce, we have to find ways to laugh alone. Sometimes this can be difficult because serious people tend to want other people to be serious as well, and they work to make them that way.

One thing solemn people use to try to keep people around them serious is control. They often do this by criticizing their partners for approaching things lightly and attempt to engender guilt about what they consider childish behavior. They refuse to enjoy themselves, and they make it difficult for their partners to enjoy things by imposing their glum attitude on everything and by their refusal to participate in fun activities. They often refuse to spend money on pleasure, and they turn a situation that could be joyful, like the purchase of a new house for instance, into a huge, serious responsibility.

Laughter of any kind disturbs the serious ones because, unknown to them, it stirs their own biological need to laugh. Laughter is contagious, and when we are around laughter, we instinctively want to laugh also. Therefore, people who don't want to laugh have to remove laughter from their surroundings. The laughing ones who happen to have a rigid, serious partner who doesn't want to laugh have to work hard to allow themselves to laugh anyway despite their partner's disapproval and desire to control. That is not always easy to do, but any added effort required is well worth it. Who knows? If one laughs around them enough, the somber partners may lighten up a little in spite of themselves.

The Search for Laughter Reborn

> In this world, a good time to laugh is any time you can.
> —Linda Ellerbee

Fortunately, when she decided to laugh again, Andrea did not focus on changing Ted's reluctance to laugh. She focused on herself. Once she made her decision to regain her laughter, she began to look for ways to laugh without Ted. She thought she might find some answers on the

Internet, and that is where she began her search. Andrea did not go searching for humor. Although she enjoyed humor, she knew from experience that she needed more than jokes. Therefore, she went looking for facts and information about laughter.

Among the more informative web sites on laughter, she found this author's web site on Laughter Therapy. She found the information about laughter both helpful and hopeful because it offered ideas about incorporating laughter into one's daily life as a natural coping mechanism. That was right up Andrea's alley. She decided to purchase a book written by this author called *The Belly Laughter Workbook*. She needed specific ideas and tools to help her laugh. The workbook provided self-tests and techniques designed to increase laughter in dealing with everyday issues in relationships like money, communication, and power struggles.

In her campaign to laugh more, Andrea began to utilize the ideas she found in the book by making only slight modifications to make them work for her as one person laughing instead of a couple. In addition to using techniques from the book, she also decided to accept a friend's suggestion to go for individual counseling with a professional laughter therapist who could help her work, with laughter, on her disturbing feelings about her relationship.

As she began to learn more about laughter, Andrea was impressed to find out that laughter relates to the release of emotional pain, and that is why it provides balance and perspective when dealing with normal but difficult things. That made sense to Andrea who recalled laughing with her family about many things that weren't funny. She also found she felt better emotionally after taking just a few, beginning steps to regain the laughter she had given up over the years.

Andrea found she enjoyed immersing herself in laughter again. As she learned about the need for laughter in relationships in order to keep them vital and healthy, she realized she had stopped approaching life with laughter when she and Ted bogged down in the basic power struggle over getting their own needs met. As they homed in on asking, "What's in it for me?" instead of "How can I make my partner feel loved?" the seriousness of the issues became paramount, and she somehow lost her appreciation for the absurd. She found it astonishing in retrospect how numb seriousness could make her feel and how controlling it could be. She had allowed her once carefree spirit that had always winked at life to become totally caught up in the serious responsibilities of marriage like housework, savings accounts, and buying assets like the house and cars.

As Andrea began to explore her marriage from an individual perspective, she was able to step back from the fighting and the unhappiness. She began to see how silly many of the things they fought over really were. In her counseling with me, she began to work to develop a lighter way of looking at her issues. She struggled with such things as standing up for herself, asking for what she needed, and developing a sense of self. Andrea slowly began to regain her ability to think differently about her problems. She had once been practically famous among her friends and family for her quirky view of things, and she was delighted to see it resurface.

Utilizing this different way of thinking in her quest for new ways to handle things, Andrea decided to compose a funny, short poem entitled, "How Can I Love Thee When Thou Art so Serious?" She giggled as she worked and found herself laughing at the finished product. As a result, the importance of Ted's serious nature shrank a little.

Andrea also worked to create ways to play with her misery, so she might see solutions to her problems she had missed before. For example, as she entertained herself with a visual image of herself staggering under a backpack labeled "Serious Ted," she realized she could actually smile about it. Her smile indicated to her that she could let go of her need to make Ted a different person. As she dropped her need to change Ted, she found herself planning outings with her friends instead of feeling she had to stay home with Ted all the time. Why, oh why, she wondered, haven't I given myself permission to do this before? In her imagination, a booming voice from the heavens said, "Because in serious relationships, couples think they are seriously joined at the hip and can't do things apart. Go, my child, and have a nice, unserious day." Chuckling to herself, Andrea set up an evening with friends.

In addition to using her own imagination, Andrea used many of the exercises in the workbook to develop ways to handle things differently. She began moving toward issues instead of running away from them, and as she jumped off each new cliff, the drop seemed to become shorter and shorter. She was no longer afraid of Ted's disapproval and no longer felt a need to defend her laughter. As she changed the ways she interacted with Ted, she slipped out of the ongoing power struggle with him and found it easier to avoid that trap than it had been in the past. She began having more fun in her life in spite of the fact that her relationship was not ever going to qualify as a "barrel of laughs."

One of the ways Andrea began having more fun in her difficult relationship was to look at the good things about having a serious husband. For example, she decided Ted's seriousness made her look like a very witty, pleasant companion. Other people saw Ted as very lucky to have a wife who was such fun. Andrea also decided it was a positive that she was finally able to decide when and where to be playful without consulting Ted. His never opting to be playful really set her free.

As she gave herself permission to laugh and have fun in spite of her serious husband, she also found it easier to feel okay about herself whether Ted approved or not. When she could feel his disapproval weighing down on her, she began repeating to herself, "Laughter is a good thing. Laughter is a good thing. Laughter is a good thing." It became her mantra and minimized the weight of his disapproval.

On the occasions when Andrea still found herself caught in a power struggle with Ted in spite of her best efforts, she would remind herself to take the initiative and try to over-fill his unmet need. If, for example, he complained that she was not affectionate enough, she would go on spurts of being so affectionate for twenty-four hours that he stopped complaining and actually backed off a little. Andrea also helped herself get out of the power struggle by developing comical, internal images of Ted that helped her cope with arguments more easily. When he was griping about something she didn't agree with, she visualized him sitting there in a rabbit suit, nibbling on a carrot, and talking away in a Bugs Bunny voice. Somehow, it was harder to get upset with a giant rabbit than it was with Ted. Therefore, most of the time, she could stay calm and respond to his issues more sensibly.

In addition to the other things she was doing, Andrea began to incorporate more humor in her days by any means possible. She looked for humor around her in cartoons, advertising signs, and human behavior. She learned to appreciate the quips by others made directly to her or ones that she might overhear. She watched television programs that were light and helped her laugh, and she started going to movies that were positive, funny, and uplifting. She no longer begged Ted to go with her. She went with friends instead. She also consciously developed more friends who laughed a lot and who appreciated her own laughter and sense of humor.

Andrea began to deliberately say positive and upbeat things to her husband. She stopped trying to convince him to be more positive, and she no longer tried to make him laugh. She learned that trying to make people laugh when they don't want to laugh feels controlling and irritating to them, and they are less likely to laugh than before. Andrea also stopped defending herself when Ted criticized her "Pollyanna" or "silly" attitude. She simply reminded herself that his opinion was only an opinion. Every time she said that to herself, she thought, That sounds like a quote by Yogi Berra—a thought that made her smile.

As Andrea loosened up her interaction in her relationship, she found she could once again enjoy the crazy, absurd things happening in her life and in the world around her. She talked and laughed with family members more, and she laughed heartily at her own humor again. She found herself to be entertaining, and that added fun to her life.

Andrea accepted the fact that she was not able to be one hundred per cent lighthearted about her marriage, and found there were still times when she yearned for a partner who would laugh and play with her. However, having ways to laugh more herself kept her from feeling tense and trapped in her marriage. She tried to focus more on the good things about Ted than on his shortcomings. It helped to remember what she liked about him initially, and she tried to stay focused on those qualities instead of the qualities that drove her crazy. She stopped trying to see either Ted or herself as right or wrong and saw them both as doing the best they could instead.

Focus on Your Own Laughter

Humor is your own smile surprising you in the mirror.
—Langston Hughes

For people like Andrea who want to laugh, it is possible to use laughter and humor to improve the quality of life and one's relationship without the partner's cooperation and involvement. In order to do this, the focus must move from the partner's inability to laugh and play to one's own ability to laugh and play without him or her. If a person stays focused on making the partner laugh or lighten up, a power struggle inevitably takes place that will suck any fun that remains right out of the relationship. Criticizing one another's laughter, sense of humor and playfulness adds sourness to any power struggle and will only increase the difficulty in finding resolution. A struggle over laughter is more serious than a power struggle over anything else. It somehow strikes at the core of one's sense of identity and makes a person feel defective on a deeply personal and unchangeable level. Therefore, laughter and one's sense of humor should be off limits to criticism.

If you want to be a laughing individual, it is important to give yourself permission to laugh whether your partner approves or not. You need to find ways to weave laughter into all those serious issues like love, approval, money, or sex all by yourself. It is possible to amuse yourself in many little ways that do not need input from others. Sara, for example, slips a grin into her day each morning as she takes her vitamins. She asks herself, "B-2 or not B-2? That is the question." Then she smiles at the silliness of it all. The fact that her husband has pronounced it "dumb" doesn't faze her one bit. She finds it fun, and that is all that matters.

Laughter Doesn't Change the Facts—It Changes the Way We Relate to the Facts

Humor is the ability to see three sides of one coin.
—Ned Rorem

The issues in relationships may be large or small, but they are all open to laughter if you put it there, even if you laugh alone. Brie, for example, was a woman with a serious problem that she had to laugh about alone. She had a husband who was ultra tight with money. She ultimately had to give up on getting him to ease up about spending. He was serious about money and could not bear to part with it. It made her crazy.

Finally, in self-defense, she decided to adopt a fun approach to her money problem with her less-than-generous spouse. She began to amuse herself by saying to one or two trusted friends, "My husband is so tight he can squeeze a fart out of a buffalo nickel." She visualized him squeezing those farts out one after another until she could laugh about it. She could even see the buffalo with its tongue hanging out from all the squeezing. As a final touch, she started singing, "Oh give me a home where the buffalo don't roam," and found it added to her laughter. All of this helped change the way she related to the rather serious facts of the problem. Once she developed a more balanced perspective about the issue, it was easier to live with it.

In addition to deliberately weaving laughter into things like Brie and Sara, you can also laugh more if you avoid taking everything to heart. You will be better able to do this if you make sure to remember that under normal circumstances you have equal power to your spouse. Neither partner in a relationship can force the other to his will just because he or she wants to do so. Just recognizing this fact is empowering and can help you work with your partner to find a mutually satisfying way to cope with your serious differences. Instead of accepting something you don't like and allowing your anger to smolder, you can speak up and ask for what you think is more acceptable.

Seeing yourself as equal to your partner makes dealing with your feelings easier. If, for example, your partner makes you angry about something like taking a vacation, you can handle your anger effectively by having a satisfying tantrum away from him or her. You can hit a pillow, stomp around the block with his or her name on the bottom of your shoes, or smash a tiny, imaginary version of your partner on the table. Anything that works for you as a release for anger is okay as long as it doesn't hurt anyone else. If you want to deal with your anger less directly, a lighter way to cope with your feelings about the vacation would be saying to yourself, "Vacation, Hee, Hee." Say it several times and you will find the issue is smaller and no longer seems hopeless. If you say "Vacation, Hee, Hee" aloud, you may laugh aloud.

Even if you don't laugh because of these techniques, the fact that they help you think funnier will help you feel different and can change your perspective about the issue. It is especially helpful if you enjoy your own sense of humor. After using a laughter technique to help you deal with your anger, you can go back to your partner and discuss an issue again when you are calmer and more open to a compromise. You will have a much better chance at success.

Another way to increase your laughter and use it to improve the quality of your relationship without your partner's participation is to take the techniques discussed throughout this book and use them by yourself. For example, if you catch yourself feeling whiny, exaggerate it to yourself. Moan a little. Ham it up. You can do this in your imagination or aloud when you are alone, so you won't irritate your partner. It will still change your perspective effectively and help you feel better.

Another example of using a laughter technique in your relationship without your partner's involvement is to thank your partner for his or her good deeds with a lighthearted "Thank you, thank you, thank you, thank you." Demand no response. The playfulness involved will help you feel like you are having fun. Your partner does not have to play for it to work for you.

If you need to loosen up your own sexual tension in your relationship, you can allow yourself to laugh discretely when that sexual technique you're trying doesn't quite work the way you'd planned. Discretely is the operative word in this case. You don't want to hurt your partner's feelings by laughing aloud at the wrong time, and you certainly don't want to laugh and point.

There are many other ways similar to the ones mentioned

here that will help you amuse yourself both openly and within the privacy of your own mind. You only need to tap into your imagination. You can use most laughter techniques alone to amuse yourself, and life will be so much more enjoyable when you see humor in it. Even the most serious things can be amusing if we are open to the idea that laughter is not demeaning. After all, according to James Thurber, "Laughter need not be cut out of anything since it improves everything."

A Relationship Is Possible When Only One Person Laughs

We are all here for a spell.
Get all the good laughs you can.
—Will Rogers

In trying to laugh more without your partner's help, it is helpful to realize that you are working on childhood issues with your spouse and that he or she is most likely unaware of what is happening. If you are aware that an issue isn't necessarily about the present, you can look more clearly at what is driving you crazy. Achieving distance from the issue will allow you to see things a little less seriously and laugh more easily. According to Harvey Mindess, author of *Laughter and Liberation,* laughter itself enables us to stand above an issue, acknowledge it, and treat it lightly in the awareness that we are touched by the issue but not contained by it. Therefore, if an issue does not control us, the humor lurking within may become more apparent. For example, you may see how humorous it is to try to yell someone into being calm.

In addition to helping you find humor in situations that aren't funny, having some distance from the situation can also enable you to look for the good things in your relationship instead of focusing on the negatives. If you choose to do this, the feelings of approval you develop will cause it to matter less that your relationship is so serious.

Nevertheless, even with the stuffiest partners, you can always find out what he or she perceives as fun. Then, try to get your partner to have fun with you in ways that do not require him or her to be particularly silly or playful. Serious people will often participate in organized fun that isn't silly or uncontrolled because they don't feel so threatened by their vulnerability.

It's not terribly difficult to find pleasurable activities that require very little risk of undue silliness. For example, we have lots of movies, plays, computer games, and professional sports events from which to choose. We have a great deal of passive fun available in our society because, as a group, Americans tend to be passive humor and fun consumers. We are afraid of being vulnerable in silliness. Your partner may be a passive consumer, but he or she might participate in the fun if they are not at risk of looking or feeling silly and out of control.

It is possible for couples to have a good relationship even if one of them insists on a rather solemn existence. Although laughter makes it much easier for most people to relate, trying to loosen up is a form of purgatory for some. That does not mean they can't be a good, lifetime companion. Partners just have to accept each other's differences in their approach to life and focus on appreciating strengths that don't relate to laughter and humor.

Andrea, for example, found that as her own laughter returned and she developed better ways to approach her relationship and life itself more lightheartedly, she began to feel better personally. She didn't need Ted to respond to life exactly as she did. She could look at him more objectively and actually feel compassion for Ted's need to stay serious all the time. His heavy-handed approach to things still annoyed her at times, and she really had to work to lighten up. However, each time she succeeded, it became easier.

For his part, Ted found it increasingly difficult to resist the appeal of Andrea's laughter. Even though it disturbed

168 / ENDA JUNKINS

him and he couldn't join in, it also loosened something wound up very deep inside him, and he enjoyed being with her again even if he didn't show it much. He still tried to make her more serious at times but gave up when she refused to fight about it. Even though Ted was afraid to join her fun, he appreciated being around it and responded to it deep inside and the relationship improved.

As the relationship improved and despite the fact that Andrea still found herself occasionally wishing Ted were more fun, she discovered she could love and appreciate him as he was, seriousness and all. At times, she even modified her own need to be silly and laugh out of respect for his feelings. In his turn, as he accepted his inability to control her laughter, he became somewhat less caustic and critical of her less serious approach to life. Because of her changes and his, the tension in Andrea's jaws finally relaxed, and the joy she felt because of her individual campaign to laugh enabled her to stay with Ted without feeling trapped.

Andrea and Ted are not a rare combination in couples. It's an interesting fact that serious people are often attracted to people who are playful, funny, and lighthearted and vice versa. The attraction is an instinctive need for balance. For the stoic person, it is perhaps a yearning to be less serious, and for the lighthearted partner, it is a need to have his or her wit appreciated and balanced by the partner's no-nonsense approach.

No matter how great the initial attraction, however, serious people tend to be controlled in their approach to life, and after they make a long-term commitment, they often feel a need to stifle their previous tolerance for people and things less serious. This need causes them to work to change their partners into serious people like them. The lighthearted partners see this rejection of their behavior as criticism. They begin to feel angry, and they yearn for someone to appreciate them and laugh with them. They also become critical of their partner's seriousness, and the relationship slips into a troubled state of affairs.

Therefore, to save relationships when seriousness narrows in on lightheartedness, people who want to laugh must fight to maintain their laughter. Not only individuals but also our society discounts things that aren't serious because we deem them unimportant. Society perceives people who laugh about serious things as irresponsible and frivolous. Consequently, lighthearted people have to resist both their serious partner's disapproval and society's disapproval if they are to keep their laughter and fun and maintain the relationship.

People who keep laughing when they have a serious partner must believe in laughter and know that it does not preclude being a responsible adult. If you are such a person, believe in yourself, believe in your laughter, and believe in your own equality to all the serious people in the world. Resist being sucked under by the serious quicksand of existence. When your laughter is questioned, support yourself with the wisdom of Will Rogers who said, "We're all going to be here a spell so get all the good laughs you can."

Exercise

Liberated Laughing

Stand in front of a mirror and look seriously at your face. Then, begin to practice different smiles—big ones, little ones, crooked ones, quick ones, long ones, pretty ones silly ones. You may even throw in what some refer to as a "shit-eating grin." After smiling, begin to practice laughs. Pretend you are an actor and need to laugh for a part you are playing. Try short laughs, loud laughs, titters, chuckles, cackles, and snorts. Work at laughing until you feel it become real. You are now a "liberated laugher." Once you laugh for real, you can do it again. You can laugh at will. Enjoy laughing with yourself every morning. Although it's generally more fun to laugh with other people, laugh alone and have fun doing that too. Notice how positively it affects your day.

We don't laugh because we're happy—
we're happy because we laugh.
—William James

"Let's start our morning workout
by stretching those laugh muscles."

Chapter 7

Laugh Together Each Day and Your Partner Will Stay

Even if laughter were nothing more
than sheer silliness and fun,
it would still be a precious boon.
But we now know that it is far more than that,
that it is, in fact,
an essential element in emotional health.
—Steve Allen

This is a book about laughter and its vital role in relationships. You have received helpful information about laughter as it relates to you and your partner, and you have shared the stories of people who found ways to regain their laughter and fun. You've also been given some exercises along the way to help you and your partner laugh more. However, since all of us can benefit from as many specific tools as we can find, this chapter will provide even more exercises to help you develop a relationship that is laughter-fit and toned. Make the decision to join the people in the book and use these exercises to deliberately learn to laugh more in your relationship.

The Weekly Laughter Workout

"Life is too important to be taken seriously."
—Oscar Wilde

Creating more laughter in your relationship and your lives takes conscious effort on a daily basis. If you don't "work out" your laughter muscles, you will remain laughter lazy and serious. Ironically, it's much easier to be serious than it is to laugh a lot. However, laughter is more fun. Once you get in the habit of a daily workout, it will become a part of you and your lives together. Then, it will cease to be work. The following set of exercises will give you a laughter workout for each day of the week. Done routinely, they will help you flex your laughter muscles without the use of steroids, spinach, or other muscle-building aids.

MONDAY
Fill Yourself with Laughter

Because we live in a negative culture, most of us wake up with negative thoughts on our minds. If we don't have negative thoughts of our own, we get them from the news or from other people. Thinking negative thoughts causes our thymus glands to shrink and pump fewer disease-fighting hormones into our bodies. Negative thinking also drains our energy and increases our stress. All of these things can make us cranky and irritable with our partners. Filling ourselves with laughter, however, makes it difficult, if not impossible, to be cranky and irritable. Laughter creates a sense of well-being and a positive attitude. It also causes the body's immune system to be more effective and energizes the body as well. Therefore, you want to fill yourself with laughter on Monday in order to start the week right. You can fill yourself up by doing the following exercise:

When you awaken on Monday morning, before you get out of bed, turn off the snooze alarm and do the following visualization. Imagine yourself surrounded by the color of laughter. That color is whatever you instinctively need it to be. Then, begin breathing in slowly and deeply. Imagine your body filling up with the color of laughter and, as it does, feel yourself growing lighter and lighter. Imagine all the stressful things in your life as a turbulent ocean. See yourself floating above it laughing wildly. As you examine each stressor in the ocean, laugh spontaneously. Eventually, all the stressors fall into their proper place in their proper size, and you laugh even more freely. The ocean is now calm.

Floating there, laughing at life, you are aware of your partner floating beside you. Laughter and color flow between you and the musical sounds of your laughter fill the air. You take your partner's hand and, together, you begin the week laughing at all the serious things it may bring you. Because you are filled with laughter, it is almost impossible to be cranky with each other or to think negative thoughts. You are filled with laughter, and you tell yourself it will stay with you all through the week.

TUESDAY
Laughter Training to Laugh More

Since we tend to take laughter for granted, we need to be specific about ways to increase laughter in our relationships. In addition to creating ways to laugh more together, we need to discipline ourselves to do the things we create. Just as people use personal trainers for physical fitness, you may want a trainer for laughter. You can train each other if you are good laughers or ask a laughing friend or co-worker to offer you training. You may even ask a child. Children are great laughers, and they are creative in creating laughter and fun. Laughter training involves practicing laughter, and that is all. To arrive at the Carnegie Hall of laughter, you need to practice, practice, practice.

As the first step toward greater laughter fitness, make a list of ways to laugh more in your relationship. Discipline yourself to do at least three or four items per day with your partner. Below is a list of suggestions to get you started. Please add to your own list. Try different things. Take the things that don't work for you off the list and keep adding new ones. Your list should be dynamic and effective. Work with it each Tuesday. Remember, *you must do the things on the list* for this to work. Discipline, tee hee.

Laughter Tips for Relationships

1. Laugh together for 5 minutes each morning.

2. Do one loving and lighthearted thing for each other each day.

3. Point out the day's absurdities to each other.

4. Seek out the humor in serious situations and share it with each other.

5. Put more fun into sex. Practice fun ideas together and see what works.

6. Consciously smile at each other more.

7. Stay playful in your interaction by keeping your voices and body language playful.

8. Renew your "real vows" once a week. (See The Belly Laughter Workbook.)

9. Take turns being responsible for the humorous "thought for the day."

10. Giggle together right before going to sleep.

11. Play "Teasing Telephone Tag" by leaving outrageous messages.

12. Have a laughter match to see who can laugh loudest and longest.

13. Surround yourself with flowers. "The earth laughs in flowers." Emerson.

14. Practice laughing without control. (Spit out food: wet your pants: wet each other's pants.)

15. Echo each other's laugh. Laugh each time your partner laughs.

16. Count the number of times you laugh each day. Compete and share results.

17. Tell each other how much you enjoy the other's laughter and sense of humor.

18. Develop a fictional phone menu where you press body parts for different laughs. Press nose for giggles, press lips for chuckles, press breast for titters, etc.

19. List the positive things in your day each day and read them to each other.

20. Play together one hour a week. Examples: sing,

dance, race each other, give exaggerated hugs, count smiling faces when driving together.

WEDNESDAY
Hump Day

We all know that Wednesday is considered Hump Day for the workweek. Make it "Hump Day" for your relationship as well. It's a good day to set aside for a little playful sex. Create a Hump Day for yourselves by doing the following things:

First, play the following game while getting dressed in the morning. One person asks the questions, and the other answers. Then, you reverse roles and repeat the questions.

1. How much do you love me?
   a. A whole world full.
   b. Two whole worlds full.
   c. A universe full.
   d. A galaxy full.

2. What do you find sexiest about me?
   a. My kisses.
   b. My body parts.
   c. My lovemaking skills.
   d. My creative approach to lovemaking.

3. How shall we begin tonight?
   a. With a kissing contest.
   b. With a shared bath.
   c. With a sensual dinner.
   d. With something naughty (like skinny dipping, making love in the car, dressing up in a fantasy).

4. How can we put fun into Hump Day?
   a. By making suggestive phone calls to each other.

  b. By wearing clown noses during the preliminaries to lovemaking.
  c. By warming up with explicit emails to one another.
  d. By singing love songs together.

 5. Will you still respect me in the morning if I:
  a. Love you with unbridled passion?
  b. Adore you more than yesterday?
  c. See you as the sexiest person I know?
  d. Desire you more each day?

In the evening, begin the intimate festivities with something creative. For example, you might try kissing each other the way you imagine famous lovers might kiss. Rhett Butler's kiss might be strong, deliberate, and delicious. Marilyn Monroe's kiss might be breathless, full-bodied, and giggly. Leonardo de Caprio may kiss with great charm and sensitivity. Julia Roberts may delight with passion and humor as she kisses. You can add fun by dressing the part, at least partially. Rhett, for instance, might have on a top hat and nothing else. Marilyn might wear a seductive teddy. Allow your theme and your creativity to continue as you enjoy letting your fun-filled intimacy ease you over the hump.

THURSDAY
I Love You When You Are Irritating

As the week winds down, you may need to lighten up about your partner's irritating behaviors. Begin doing this by making a list of the things your partner does that irritate you. You can use the following checklist to get started and add your own particular irritations if they are not on this list.

1. You irritate me when you criticize me.
2. You irritate me when you don't remember to pick up the items at the store.
3. You irritate me when you are late.
4. You irritate me when you interrogate me.
5. You irritate me when you aren't more like me.
6. You irritate me when you don't help me without my asking.
7. You irritate me when you don't clean up after yourself.
8. You irritate me when you cling to me.
9. You irritate me when you ignore me.
10. You irritate me when you don't listen.
11. You irritate me when you don't admire me.
12. You irritate me when you interrupt me.

After creating your list, take each item and identify what you think about each thing that creates your irritation. Then, choose to think about the irritating behavior in a funny way. After doing this, try to be angry about the behavior and see what happens. It will be virtually impossible to be irritated by it because your perspective will have changed. It may be too difficult to do all the behaviors at once, so do two at a time each week until you do them all. Use the following example to get the hang of changing your thoughts.

When you criticize me, my serious thoughts are: There you go again. I never do anything right. I feel like you don't love me as I am.

You can change those thoughts to light or humorous thoughts like: There you go again, you criticizing devil you. Even when you're criticizing me you're a cute little thing. We have equal power, you know, so your criticism can just go to the moon for all I care. Your criticisms just make me appreciate your compliments all the more, and I am even more certain that you love me.

When you change your thoughts and lighten them up, you will feel more secure, more positive, and more empowered. Laughter and humor can be an emotional form of the martial arts by taking the energy from critical comments and robbing them of their power. They will also deflect criticism from its target. Therefore, you no longer have to feel unsafe with your partner.

FRIDAY
The Laughter Sanctuary

Whew! The week is over, and you may have returned home a bit battered and bruised from events taking place during the week. On Fridays, you need to come home to a laughter sanctuary. First, however, you need to create one together. To create a laughter sanctuary, try the following things:

1. Choose a space for your sanctuary. It can be a whole room or a part of a room.

2. Include humorous items in your decor for the sanctuary. For example, hang a framed cartoon on the wall. Get a few humorous knick-knacks for the area and put a few stress relieving toys around.

3. Arrange access to canned laughter from a CD, audiotape, videotape, or laugh boxes to be enjoyed in your sanctuary.

4. Start collecting funny sayings, incidents from everyday life, items from the newspaper, light advertisements, etc. Make a file or scrapbook to contain them and go through them every Friday in the sanctuary.

5. Sit together in your sanctuary and share with each other the funny things that you heard, saw, or experienced during the week.

6. Look at each other and smile for a minute or two. Don't talk to each other, just smile. Then, laugh a little together.

7. Make a rule that the laughter sanctuary is only for laughter. No one may be serious in the laughing place.

You can use your laughter sanctuary together or use it alone if you wish. It is a very good place to destress and depressurize from the week. It is also a good place to talk positively about things or to end an argument. Laughter creates positive attitudes, and it creates safety. No one should be without a laughter sanctuary.

SATURDAY
The Laughter Reflection

We all need to reflect at times, and most of us do far too little reflection. If we don't take time to reflect on the serious things in our lives, how much less do we reflect on the humorous things? Take a few minutes to reflect on the things you like about the ways you and your partner share laughter. It will not only urge you to smile and laugh together more, it will remind you of how much fun you both are and how much you enjoy being together.

The following exercise should help you identify what your partner does that makes you laugh.

The number one thing most people seek in a partner is a sense of humor. People also believe it's very important to have a sense of humor themselves. Although people can laugh about things that aren't funny, shared humor certainly adds laughter to a relationship. Do you and your partner share humor with one another? Check all that apply.

_____ My partner is always saying funny things.

_____ We like the same kind of comedies.

_____ We laugh about the same things in everyday life.

_____ When I think about my partner's sense of humor, I smile.

_____ We don't criticize each other for laughing.

_____ We share a good joke with each other when we hear one.

_____ We actively look for humor in life and share it.

_____ Our families have similar senses of humor.

_____ We enjoy the same type of comedians on TV.

_____ My partner laughs at my attempts to be funny.

_____ We use humor to help us communicate.

_____ We enjoy similar humor in greeting cards.

_____ We like the same type of funny slogans on T-shirts and other similar items.

_____ The differences in our senses of humor actually make us funnier to each other.

_____ We use humor to cope with serious things.

_____ Our shared humor makes us feel closer to one another emotionally.

If you checked at least five items, you and your partner share some humor with each other. Five or more and humor plays an important role in your lives together. If you checked none of the above, you and your partner may want to work on adding some humor to your relationship.

Reflect on the things you checked for a moment and then close your eyes. Imagine yourself surrounded by your partner's smiles, laughs, chuckles and humor. See your own smiles, laughs, chuckles, and humor mingling with his or hers. Then, imagine yourself drenched in sunshine and surrounded by all this laughter. Revel in it for a moment and then, open your eyes. Look at your partner and notice how he or she looks to you now. Note how you feel. Share your feelings with your partner so he or she can experience your appreciation.

SUNDAY
Toning Up Your Week

One of the most common triggers for arguments among couples is tone of voice. Couples accuse each other with, "It's not what you say, but how you say it!" If asked for clarification, the accuser usually says, "It's your tone of voice." They are generally unable to be more specific, so the accused feels confused about what to do about the situation. If there is no clear description of the negative tone, how does one change it?

The issue is a real one because we do convey feeling in our tone of voice. However, to communicate clearly with one another about our feelings, we need to be able to identify those infamous tones. We have all been disciplined for a negative tone of voice as children, and we respond to one another with all the hurt from childhood when our tone is criticized as an adult. In order to work with this issue and set the tone for a good week, the following exercise is a good beginning for your weekly laughter workout.

Below, you will find a list of the most common tones of voice that get us into trouble with one another and those that do not. Check the tones you and your partner tend to use with one another.

Negative		Positive	
1. ___	Angry	1. ___	Sweet
2. ___	Impatient	2. ___	Concerned
3. ___	Condescending	3. ___	Sincere
4. ___	Whiny	4. ___	Amused
5. ___	Manipulative	5. ___	Pleasant
6. ___	Ridiculing	6. ___	Confident
7. ___	Harsh	7. ___	Warm
8. ___	Unbelieving	8. ___	Loving
9. ___	Indifferent	9. ___	Seductive
10. ___	Pleading	10. ___	Soothing
11. ___	Interrogating	11. ___	Interested
12. ___	Irritated	12. ___	Admiring

After checking off all that you use (feel free to add to the list on your own), demonstrate for each other what the particular tones sound like to you. Make it a game by choosing a tone and demonstrating it. Have your partner guess which tone it is. Keep score, and the person with the most right answers wins. Provide a prize that works for the two of you like choosing the next TV show, the next meal, or the next video to watch.

LAUGH TOGETHER EACH DAY AND YOUR PARTNER WILL STAY / 185

After establishing the sounds of the various tones, try doing each tone together. For example, do angry tones together, condescending tones together, seductive tones together. After each tone, laugh together. See how it affects your feelings about each tone. The negative tones will be less powerful, and the positive tones will be more positive and more fun.

Finally, choose the positive tone you want to be the tone of the week. If it is the pleasant tone, for example, you will both strive to use a pleasant tone with each other all week. If you slip into other tones, apologize and go back to working on using the tone of the week. Over time, you will use more positive tones and will better identify the feelings in the negative ones. Your communication will also improve. At the close of the exercise, congratulate each other for setting the right tone for the week.

Tools, Glorious Tools, More Tools

Laughter can be more satisfying than honor;
more precious than money;
more heart cleansing than prayer.
—Harriet Rochlin

In addition to your weekly laughter workout, you may want additional tools to enhance the laughter in your relationship and your lives. More exercises follow that will help you do exactly that.

Laughing and Loving

Laughter plays a major role in our attraction to one another and in our ability to stay in love. Without fail, people desire laughter and a sense of humor in their partners. Without laughter, it's hard to enjoy one another. Complete the following inventory to identify the importance of laughter in your relationship.

	Yes	No
1. One major reason I was attracted to my partner was because of the laughter.	___	___
2. When I laugh with my partner, I feel fully present in the moment.	___	___
3. Laughter makes it easier for us to cope with difficult issues or situations	___	___
4. Laughter helps us enjoy life together even more.	___	___
5. Laughter eases conflict so we can work things out.	___	___
6. We use laughter and play to make everyday chores more bearable.	___	___
7. I feel closer to my partner when we laugh together.	___	___
8. Laughter adds a little extra zip to our love for each other.	___	___
9. Laughter helps us "go with the flow" when life throws us lemons.	___	___
10. My partner and I often laugh about things that are serious.	___	___

	Yes	No
11. Laughter adds to my anticipation of time with my partner.	____	____
12. When I laugh with my partner, I feel my love for him/her more deeply.	____	____

People who laugh together, last together. If you answered yes to at least nine of the statements above, you are well on your way to a rollicking good time together for years to come.

Laugh Along with Me

One of the best feelings in the world is to have the person we love most think we are witty and fun. Most of us enjoy this in the beginnings of our relationships and can do so throughout the relationship with just a little added effort. Do you find your partner funny? Does he or she find you funny? Use the following exercise to explore these questions.

Make a list of the areas and ways in which you find your partner funny.

1.

2.

3.

4.

5.

Make a list of areas and ways in which you believe he or she finds you funny.

1.

2.

3.

4.

5.

How many times a day do you and your spouse laugh? _____

Fill in the following blanks.

1. You have to have a _____ to laugh.

2. _____ and humor are the same thing.

3. We laugh when we are _____.

If you put reason, laughter, and happy as your answers, you just defined the three myths about laughter. The truth is that we laugh because we hurt emotionally, and laughter releases anger, fear, and boredom. We do not need a reason to laugh. Hopefully, you and your partner will try to laugh now as much as you did at four years old when you laughed five hundred times a day. Relearn the art of laughing for no real reason at all. You'll be happier as a result.

We Laugh Because We Hurt

Laughter is such a good thing. It makes us feel wonderful, but few of us know why. Laughter makes us feel good because it releases three painful emotions: fear, anger, and boredom. It's hard for many people to know what they're feeling, and that difficulty makes it virtually impossible to share feelings with their partners. Releasing feelings and then talking about them with our partners is essential in a good relationship. Can you identify your feelings? Feelings are variations on the intensity of emotions. Can you relate your feelings to one of the three major emotions released by laughter: fear, anger, and boredom? Use the following list to help you identify your feelings and relate them to laughter and the painful emotions.

For example: Worry is the feeling, and fear is the emotion.

Feeling	Emotion
Exhausted	_____
Confused	_____
Suspicious	_____
Guilty	_____
Angry	_____
Hysterical	_____
Frustrated	_____
Embarrassed	_____
Disgusted	_____
Frightened	_____
Enraged	_____
Ashamed	_____

Feeling	Emotion
Cautious	_____
Depressed	_____
Overwhelmed	_____
Jealous	_____
Bored	_____
Surprised	_____
Anxious	_____
Shocked	_____
Shy	_____
Apathetic	_____
Irritated	_____
Disappointed	_____

Major positive emotions are love, joy, hope, compassion, and trust. Can you identify them in yourself?

Feeling	Emotion
Ecstatic	_____
Confident	_____
Happy	_____

Feeling	Emotion
Mischievous	_____
Hopeful	_____
Lovely	_____
Lovestruck	_____
Caring	_____
Generous	_____
Giving	_____
Sympathetic	_____
Upbeat	_____
Encouraged	_____
Tender	_____
Warm	_____

We can only feel our positive emotions if we allow ourselves to feel our painful ones. Laughter releases three of our painful emotions. If you laugh a lot with your partner, you will feel deeply as well.

Face Off

When caught in the power struggle of a relationship, we tend to fight over little things that won't really matter in the long run. They seem important at the time, and the

192 / Enda Junkins

battles over them can be "deadly serious." Dealing with such things with playful exaggeration will not only keep the problem in perspective, it can help pull up the deeper, hidden issues. Try the following exercise and see how you feel.

First, list all the little things you and your partner fight about—like the toilet seat, the toothpaste tube, or the lights on or off. Write the items here.

Now, for a good playful fight. (1) Pick the bone of contention you like best. (2) Choose the appropriate arena. A fight over the toothpaste tube should take place in the bathroom, for example. (3) Give each fighter the necessary supplies and equipment. In our example, that is a large tube of toothpaste. (4) Develop a clear set of rules, set the alarm clock, and at the sound of the bell begin the fight. In our toothpaste fight, the one to squeeze all the toothpaste from the tube first wins. (5) Add playful verbal jabs as you go along. For example, while squeezing your tube madly at the place of your choice, bottom or middle, let your partner have it verbally. For example, "I'm squeezing the tube in the middle, ha, ha, ha ha, ha (in sing song)." "My tube is neater than yours because I'm squeezing at the bottom. Bottoms are better." "My toothpaste is coming out faster because I'm squeezing in the middle." "Middle, smiddle, I'll still get all the paste out first." Keep excitement in your voices. If you can have spectators (like children), that's even better. (6) Add as many creative twists to the fight as you can.

When you stop laughing, wipe the "sweat" from your brow and consider how you feel.

Ask your partner how he or she feels.
What did you learn?
How important is the issue (of the toothpaste) now?

The Bullet Point Tantrum

Everybody gets angry now and then. It's a natural emotion that prods us to keep people out of our space. Anger, by itself, does no harm. It's how we act it out that hurts others. When you and your partner are in a power struggle for control of something, you need some quick, easy ways to have a tantrum that won't hurt the other person. Try the following suggestions and see how you feel.

1. Sit or stand and stomp your feet, wave your fists up and down and scream, "Meet my needs. Meet my needs. Meet my needs." You may do it by yourself or together, one at a time or simultaneously. It also works well for groups, so the whole family can do it together if needed.
2. Visualize a tiny version of the person or thing you are angry with. See it on a flat surface and then take your hand and smash it flat. Afterwards, thump it off the surface.
3. Take a "toy ray gun" and shoot the person, issue, or thing that is irritating you.
4. Write what you are angry about on a piece of paper and flush it.
5. Use a toy prop to vent your anger. Choke it, smash it, and throw it. Do whatever helps.
6. Take ice cubes and throw them at a wall while focusing on what you are angry about.
7. Beat the "stuffing" out of a bed with a plastic baseball bat.

Add your own ideas for "bullet point" tantrums to this list. List them here.

1.

2.

3.

4.

5.

Write down your feelings before and after your "bullet point" tantrum. Then, ask yourself—"What did I learn?"

Personal Advisor

One thing that often frustrates couples is the failure of partners to take each other's advice or accept each other's ideas. Does this frustrate you? Let the following quiz help you find out.

	Yes	No
I like to offer advice whether it's asked for or not.	____	____
I feel like my partner listens to my ideas and advice.	____	____
I feel my partner appreciates my intelligence and my problem solving abilities.	____	____
I can see the gratitude in my partner's eyes when I advise him or her.	____	____

	Yes	No
I am always grateful when they advise me.	___	___
I am smarter than the average person.	___	___
My partner is just as smart as I am.	___	___
I am completely okay when my partner doesn't follow my advice.	___	___
I would rather give advice than receive it.	___	___

If you answered no to four or more of the above questions, you experience frustration about advice. If you want to lighten up about it, you can:

1. Offer advice playfully as a famous expert.
2. You can **profusely** thank your partner for advice given and he or she can be **grandly** accepting. (Playfully exaggerate.)
3. You can list aloud playful, fictitious, tragic results if your partner fails to appreciate your ideas or advice. For example, you might predict earthquakes or horrible thunderstorms if they don't listen.

You can create any number of ways to play with this issue that work for you. If you treat ideas and advice playfully, you won't take it personally if it's not accepted or acted upon.

Talk to Me, Baby

Men and women learn different ways to communicate as they grow up. It is a crucial problem in relationships as they try to communicate with each other. Men tend to talk to women as if they were men, and women tend to talk to men as if they were women. We need to find ways to talk to our partners that are meaningful to them. Do you find yourself unable to get your message across at times? The following, lighthearted exercise can help you improve communication playfully.

If you are a woman, practice being direct and more specific and forthright in what you say. Stand before your partner, playfully hitch up your pants, scratch your crotch and say something like, "Hey man, will you give me a hand with the kids? Timmy's dirty. Will you give him a bath?"

If you are a man, practice saying reassuring things and acknowledge your partner's feelings. Try to be a little more long-winded in getting to the point. Put play into your practice. Sit down by your partner, fluff your hair, raise your voice an octave, and say something like, "How are you doing? Did you have a tough day? You poor baby. My day was stress from hell. Are you hungry? You look starved. I'm hungry too. I've had Mexican food on my mind all day long. Do you feel like Mexican food? Want to go to Don Pablo's? It'll make us both feel better, don't you think?"

Now, list five things you and your partner have problems communicating about.

1.

2.

3.

4.

5.

Use the playful approach described above to try communicating about the items on your list. Remember to exaggerate and keep it light. This should provide you and your partner with a different perspective on the issues. The laughter created will make it easier to talk to one another until you reach an understanding.

Love Letters with A Twist

Writing is a powerful way to express affection. Love letters always have a special place in your heart and in the heart of your beloved. Now, in addition to the straight-forward, romantic letters, pen a little playfulness to your partner. Use the following exercise to get started.

Create a list of all the great lovers you can think of. Examples would be Romeo and Juliet or Scarlett O'Hara and Rhett Butler. Then, write a letter to your partner as if you are one of the famous lovers you listed. Express your own feelings in terms you think they would have used. Notice how you feel as you write and share these feelings with your partner later. Be sure to find out what their feelings were as the recipient of the letter.

Example: Dear Ann, I awoke this morning to the lush smell of magnolias, and my heart lurched to think I might lose you to one of those unspeakable Yanks from the North. Atlanta hasn't been the same since....

Little Bitty Notes of Love

Notes that tell our partners we love them are always appreciated. They also lend themselves well to play. We can play with what we say and with where we leave the notes. Create a list of places to leave notes for your partner and then put together a few ideas to play with the content.

Example: Leave the note taped to the toilet seat and say something like, "You flush all the cares from my day."

List five creative places to leave notes for your partner.

1.

2.

3.

4.

5.

List an idea for the content of a note to go with each site.

1.

2.

3.

4.

5.

List five places where it would tickle your funny bone to find a note from your partner.

1.

2.

3.

4.

5.

How do you think such a note would affect your day? Your partner's day?

Share your feelings with your partner. Ask your partner to share his or her feelings about getting such loving, lighthearted notes.

Thank You, Thank You, Thank You

Many people have trouble giving and receiving compliments. This situation may be due to the fact that they grew up in families where the parents believed compliments create conceit. It may be due to low self-esteem when a person doesn't feel worthy of a compliment. Withholding compliments and approval may also be a passive-aggressive way of expressing anger. None of us got enough approval as children. None of us get enough now. Complimenting your partner creates love, laughter and safety. Do you compliment your partner enough? Do you receive enough compliments? Complete the following exercise to find out.

List five things you have complimented your partner on in the last week.

1.

2.

3.

4.

5.

List five compliments you received from your partner in the last week.

1.

2.

3.

4.

5.

What prevents you from giving compliments?

_____

What prevents you from receiving compliments graciously and gratefully? _____

Compliments are not necessarily serious. Play with giving and receiving compliments by using the following exercise:

Each partner needs to make a list of twenty things, large and small, that they like about their partner. Ten areas for compliments are listed below. Think of one specific thing you like about your partner in these areas, add ten more, and begin playing.

<u>Things I Like about My Partner</u>

1. Physical attributes—eyes, hair, body, etc.
2. Jobs well done
3. Child care
4. Travel companionship
5. Sense of humor
6. Fun
7. Financial
8. Gifts given

9. Romance
10. Sex

To play, one partner will give a compliment to the other. The other responds with an exaggerated "Thank you, thank you, thank you." Then reverse it and take turns through all twenty things.

How do you feel after giving and receiving praise?

_____

What did you learn? _____

This experience done regularly should create the desire to compliment because it's fun, and one feels loving doing it. It also will eliminate discomfort about being complimented. Compliment each other at least twice daily. Have fun!

Exaggerate Your Needs

As simple as it may seem, many partners fail to ask each other for what they need. They believe their partner should magically know what their needs are because their partner loves them. Somehow, they think love creates psychic powers where their needs are concerned. Do you ask for what you need? Use the following inventory to check.

<table>
<tr><td></td><td>Always</td><td>Sometimes</td><td>Never</td></tr>
<tr><td>1. I ask my partner for hugs.</td><td colspan="3">_____</td></tr>
<tr><td>2. I ask my partner for help.</td><td colspan="3">_____</td></tr>
<tr><td>3. I ask my partner for support.</td><td colspan="3">_____</td></tr>
</table>

	Always	Sometimes	Never

4. I tell my partner when I
   need reassurance.
   _____

5. I ask my partner for little
   favors when I need to
   feel more special.
   _____

6. I ask my partner to do
   one of my jobs when
   I'm really tired.
   _____

7. I ask my partner for sex
   when I want it.
   _____

8. I express my need for
   understanding.
   _____

9. I express my need for
   approval.
   _____

10. I request concrete indica-
    tions of appreciation when
    I need them.
    _____

11. I ask for a little pampering
    when I feel I've given all
    I can.
    _____

12. I ask for evidence of trust
    when I need it.
    _____

13. I ask for tolerance when
    I'm out of sorts.
    _____

14. I ask for patience when
    I'm behind.
    _____

If you marked ten or more "always," you and your partner communicate extremely well. If you marked seven or more "always" or "sometimes," you and your partner are average communicators and could be even better. If you marked seven or more "never," you and your partner would benefit from a little practice at communicating as soon as possible.

I Need You

The following exercise is a short, easy way to work with the expression of needs in a light way. Practice saying to each other, "I need you, I need you, I need you." Overdo it so it is fun. Once you're comfortable with that, practice saying "What I need from you is _____." Turn this into a game as well. The winner gets his or her need met in the best way possible and as soon as possible.

Sh-h-h-h, You Can't Talk About Sex

Many people are totally handicapped when it comes to resolving sexual issues because they can't talk about sex at all. Can you talk about sex with your partner? Even if you can, the following exercise will be fun and can later serve as a signal to each other for sex:

Stand and face each other. Throw both hands up in the air repeatedly while chanting softly at first, "Great sex, great sex, great sex." Build louder and louder until you reach maximum sound level and then work your way back down to a very soft tone. Remember to chant the whole time and look at each other while you chant.

After the exercise, pay attention to how you feel

about saying the word sex. Try saying the word "sex" aloud to each other and see if you're more comfortable. If you're not, repeat the exercise until you are.

Silly Sex

Sex is always more enjoyable if a couple is able to remain playful. If sex is fun, you will be drawn to it even more than you already are. To add fun to your sexual relationship, ask yourself if you are playful when having sex. If you don't already play sexually, devise some purely simple games to introduce play during those intimate moments. For example: Lie totally still while your partner kisses you all over. If you move, you lose.

Be sure to find out what games your partner likes to play. Then, create some games you will both enjoy and try them out later. Notice how you feel having simple fun while being intimate with one another. Did your attitude toward sex change any? How does it feel to think about sex in terms of play?

Mister, Can You Spare A Dime?

Money is a major area of conflict for many couples. Most of us aren't sure why it upsets us; it just does. Money can be a real problem all by itself but, very often, it is just the obvious arena where we fight over other needs. For example, money for men equals power, and money for women equals security. Do you fight about money? Despite the two major needs money relates to, it doesn't have to be a serious issue all the time. A few suggestions for playing with the issue of money are listed below. Try one or two and see how you feel.

- Stick "play money" in obvious places all over the house so money is always available if you need it.
- Have a treasure hunt.
- Fill a jar with pennies. When angry about money, count all the pennies first before trying to discuss it.
- If you're feeling insecure about money, carry the jar of pennies with you wherever you go for an entire day.
- Create humorous, pretend messages from bill collectors and leave them on your answering machine.
- Grandly buy everyone a hot dog at the convenience store when you feel a need to pay for everyone's dinner.
- Send someone $15.00 for a "steakette" dinner for two.
- Create a playful financial trust with all your "play money" buried in the back yard. Give each trustee a shovel.
- Create your own ways to play with money.

Playing with the issue of money will shrink its importance enough for you to recognize and address the real needs behind the issue.

Just You and Me and Baby Makes Three

An area around which many couples have disagreements is the children. Parents often disagree on discipline and who is responsible for various aspects of child care. The care of our children is a good place to seek and find humor on a daily basis. Do you find humor in the care of your children? Begin by sharing a humorous situation you have encountered in raising your children with your partner. Then, ask yourselves what is the most fun about having children? Talk about it in detail.

Consider each other's positives as parents. Talk about them together and make a list of each other's parenting strengths. Notice how it feels to have your partner think of you as a good parent. Ask yourselves what you could do to improve your negatives as parents. Be specific and remember to be a bit playful in creating solutions.

Do you play together with your children? _____

Why or why not? _____

Would you like a more playful attitude in your interaction with your partner as a parent? _____

How can the two of you develop some parenting humor? An example might be a cartoon of a baby in a diaper below which you write, "Shit Happens." Hang it somewhere to remind you to roll with the punches. If you have some humor you rely on regularly, write it down. Use it as a springboard to create new humor.

At the end of each fun-filled or frustrating day of parenting, join together and repeat this child's *serenity prayer*. "Forgive me for the naughty things I did today and for the things I planned but didn't get done."

Have Fun!

For various reasons, couples often stop having fun together early in relationships. The average couple spends ten minutes per week on fun or play. That's because they are in a "serious" relationship. What they seem unaware of is that without laughter and fun, relationships grow stale, and people wind up living lives of "quiet desperation." Have you and your partner stopped having fun? The following exercise can give you ideas for fun.

Make a list of ten things that are fun and mean love to

you. They do not have to be big or expensive. Have your partner make a list as well.

1.

2.

3.

4.

5.

6.

7.

8.

9.

10.

Now write under each item where and how it can be accomplished.

Stick your list and your partner's list up on a bulletin board or the bathroom mirror or somewhere else where you will be sure to see it. Make sure you do at least one thing from each list every week.

After two weeks of doing fun things, write your reactions on your list. Also, note its impact on your relationship. When couples have fun together, they laugh more, and they feel loved and loving.

What You Practice Is What You Become

Laughter releases stress and painful emotions. It keeps your body healthier. It helps you survive and cope more easily. It helps you think clearly and more creatively. It increases energy and productivity. It changes your perspective on things and creates generosity. It is fun, and it is bonding. Laughter helps you feel closer to your partner and more loving toward him or her. Do you need to laugh more? Try the following suggestions and add some ideas of your own as you go along.

1. Fake it till you make it. If you fake laughter, you will reap real physical and psychological benefits. If you fake it long enough and often enough, it will become real. You can learn to laugh at will as a "liberated laughter." All it takes is practice.
2. Buy "canned" laughter like a laugh box, a tape of positive laughter, or laughing toys. Laughter is contagious, and you'll soon laugh along.
3. Get audiotapes of people laughing and play the tapes at home and in your car. You will feel better, and your perspective will shift.
4. Enjoy the positive humor of comedians who are positive.
5. Look for humor in everyday life and share it with each other so you can both laugh.
6. You and your partner make a habit of starting the day with a good belly laugh for no particular reason at all.

7. When you are around people laughing, join in. Don't wonder why they're laughing. Go for it!
8. Take absolutely every opportunity to laugh every day.
9. If all you can do is plant a smile on your face with conscious effort, do it as often as you think of it. Your thoughts will shift and your environment will look and feel more pleasant. Others will respond to you differently and often smile back. Smiling very often leads to laughing.

All Good Things Must End

We had a seriousness of purpose.
We also believed the old saying that to
be serious doesn't mean to be solemn.
We reveled in our lack of solemnity.
—Alan Alda

As you finish reading and using this book, it is my sincere wish that there is light in your eyes, hope in your heart, and a smile on your face. I also hope you find you are armed with enough laughter tools for the present and future. Re-evaluating, renewing, and increasing the laughter in your relationship can be a stimulating experience. It can stir memories of better times when you were less encumbered with stress and responsibilities. It can also revive your ability to play with life and with each other. As a result, life together can be a glorious adventure that you embark on for the fun of it. All the obstacles in your path are just the trappings of adventure if you remember to view them that way and not let them get you down.

Now, in the spirit of that final thought as we come to the end of this grand adventure about laughter in relationships, go out and buy yourselves a couple of adventurous hats and step forth lightly to enjoy the next stage of your own epic saga together. Then, when life springs its traps on you, remember to look into the face of adversity and laugh.

The richest laugh is at no one's expense.
—Linda Loving

Laughter Therapy Order Form

Fax: (972) 255-4253. Send this form.
Telephone: Call (972) 255-LAFF (5233).
Web: Go to www.laughtertherapy.com.
Mail: Enda Junkins, 3200 N. MacArthur Blvd., Ste. 106, Irving, TX 75062

Belly Laughter in Relationships: Something Else Positive Below the Belt - $14.95 Quantity _____

Belly Laughter for Couples: Something Else Positive Below the Belt – Video (1 1/2 hrs.) - $34.95 Quantity _____
Audio - $14.95 Quantity _____

The Belly Laughter Workbook - $19.95 Quantity _____

The Power Of Laughter – Video (2 hrs.) - $39.95 Quantity _____
Audio - $24.95 Quantity _____

Laughter: The Light Solution For Stress
Video (1 hr.) - $24.95 Quantity _____
Audio - $11.95 Quantity _____

Lots of Laughter
CD - $15.00 Quantity _____ **Tape - $10.00** Quantity _____

Subtotal _____

Sales Tax: Texas residents add 8.25%.
Shipping and Handling: $20 or less-$4.95, $20.01-$40.00-$6.95, $40.01-$60.00-$8.95, $60.01-$100.00-$10.95, $100.01-$200.00-$13.95, $200.01 and over-$15.95.
Foreign Orders: Add 30% to subtotal. Then add regular shipping and handling to total.

Total _____

Name: _____

Address: _____

City: _____ **State:** _____ **Zip:** _____

Telephone: _____ **Email:** _____

Payment: _____ **Check** _____ **Visa** _____ **MasterCard** _____

Card #: _____ **Exp. Date:** _____

Name on Card: _____